Centering

Other books by Gerald Kushel:

FACT AND FOLKLORE *(co-author)*
DISCORD IN TEACHER-COUNSELOR RELATIONS

Centering
Six Steps
Toward
Inner Liberation

GERALD KUSHEL

Times
BOOKS

Published by TIMES BOOKS, a division
of Quadrangle/The New York Times Book Co., Inc.
Three Park Avenue, New York, N. Y. 10016

Published simultaneously in Canada by
Fitzhenry & Whiteside, Ltd., Toronto

Library of Congress Cataloging in Publication Data

Kushel, Gerald.
Centering: six steps toward inner liberation.

Includes index.
1. Self-actualization (Psychology) I. Title.
BF637.S4K87 1979   158′.1   79-51448
ISBN 0-8129-0856-2

Manufactured in the United States of America

Second printing, March 1980

To my dear wife, Selma
My children, Joan and Lynne
And to my father, Benjamin

ACKNOWLEDGMENTS

I wish to thank the following persons for their generous help during various phases of this work: Dr. Daniel Araoz, Dr. Stan Brodsky, Carol Engle, Sheldon Feinstein, Dr. Ed Glanz, Susan Jacobson, Karen Sacks, Phyllis Simon, Nina Sullivan, Dr. Roy Smith, and Dr. Clement Thompson. A special thanks to my editor, Roger Jellinek. In addition, I wish to express gratitude for the professional writings of Drs. Carl Rogers, Fritz Perls, and Albert Ellis, all of whom have influenced my thinking over the years. Most importantly, deep thanks to my wife, Selma, for her patience, fortitude, and support for the time taken from her for this project.

CONTENTS

Centering

Chapter
·1·
Centering

For years it was a well-kept secret, for among many of the people that I know it isn't considered very chic to be exceptionally enthusiastic about the way your life is going. Either you're lying, exaggerating terribly, or you are quite out of contact with reality. This is especially true if your outlook emerges without benefit of the latest vogue in religion or mysticism, if it is merely a result of your own thinking.

So for some time I have kept what I call my inner liberation a deep secret, living as a kind of closet hedonist. However, since I emerged from the closet, I have found that there are people around who are very much like me, many more than I had realized. Therefore, I've been able to supplement what I already understood about this lifestyle as these others added their insights to my repertoire.

It is often said, "You've got to have problems. There isn't a human being worth his salt who doesn't." There are a number of such common myths that keep many people

from having the satisfying personal existence that is everyone's birthright:

"Life wasn't meant to be easy."

"Think positive—and your troubles will go away."

"You can't help the way you feel."

"If you don't permit yourself to get angry, then you are
repressing a natural instinct."

"When things around you are brutal or complex, it's only
to be expected that you get upset and confused."

These statements, and many others like them, are utter
nonsense. Yet they are widespread and do untold damage
to millions of people, perhaps even you. This book is intended to dispel these myths once and for all.

The inner-liberated lifestyle that I explain here will enable you to enjoy a quality of inner existence that transcends any situation, no matter how unfortunate. Moreover, this way of life does not require you to "drop out,"
"turn off (or on)," "join up," or only "look out for Number
One."

The approach offered here is practical, realistic, and easily mastered by anyone who follows the six-step centering
process I describe in these pages. And what is more, this
lifestyle can be achieved without your surrendering one
iota of anything that you currently hold dear, be it family,
friends, career, or material possessions.

Sounds too good to be true, doesn't it?

Recently, a close friend of mine, an attractive person in
her early thirties who has been "single again" for the past
seven years, shared with me the sad fact that the man she
was hoping to establish a lasting relationship with had suddenly dropped her. "Abandoned again," she said despon-
dently. It was only natural that she be hurting. She told me
about the intense emotional pain and anguish she was
rightfully experiencing.

Ordinarily, as I have done many times over the years I
have known her, I would have listened sympathetically.
After all, isn't that what good friends are for—to offer warm

solace and support, especially in time of need? But I have changed. I told her, "No reason at all for you to continue to feel the way you do. Just learn to choose more effective thoughts. Rid yourself immediately of those useless feelings of depression and despair. You can do this much more rapidly than you've been led to believe. Then get on with living the satisfying life that you were put on this planet to enjoy. Don't waste an extra breath with unnecessary anguish. Wasting your life in this way offers neither you nor this world anything of value."

Needless to say, my friend became quite angry with me. "How can you say that?" she asked. "Life is just not that simple. I don't understand you anymore. Just because you've found something that works for you is no reason why you should try to impose your way of life on me. After all, Jerry, I'm me. If I feel that I need to suffer, the least you could do is to permit me to do so in peace. Please don't lecture me on how I should live. Okay?"

"It's not okay," I said. "If I didn't really care for you as much as I do, it might be okay. But I do care—very much. Look," I went on, "if I had an overweight friend who was constantly indulging himself in mashed potatoes and fried foods and desserts, would you consider me a good friend to this person if he complained to me about not being able to lose weight and I didn't tell him what I knew about dieting? Of course not, I owe him my honest opinion. And since I know that mashed potatoes, fried foods, and desserts are fattening, I feel compelled to tell him—because I care for him, not because I'm cruel or inconsiderate."

My friend began to cry. I had struck a nerve. I think she realized that I did really care about her feelings, but this time in a different way. Yet advice, I realize from my years as a therapist, is one of the poorest things to give—especially when it is unsolicited. Advice seems much too simplistic for complex human situations. Inner liberation, I've found, is easier to achieve than to talk about.

That is the main reason I have written this book. The

principles I describe here are best understood not when you are in the middle of an emotional crisis but before it occurs, and at your own leisure. What can achieve that better than a book? A book that you can read when you're interested, put down when your satiated, and pick up again —or even return to parts that were not quite clear to you the first time around—until you've mastered a position, an attitude, that can carry you readily through and beyond any hardship or complexity that life dishes up. This book, then, is for my friend—and any other person who, in a more fortunate position, can learn these principles in advance of a difficulty.

I offer no panacea for the ills of the world. No omniscient answers to the many mysteries of life. No cult or religion can be made out of what I share here. What I offer leads only to greater pluralism, greater self-sufficiency for in-dividuals—rather than anything holy, or elitist.

This is the age of the multiple bind. Instead of the mere double bind, where only two choices of equal intensity pull us in opposite directions, in these confusing times we are faced with a multiple bind, where we encounter a bewilder-ing array of options and pressures in daily living and a profusion of different guidelines from which to make our choices. A myriad of confusing "opportunities" are ham-mered into us daily through the mass media, in a way that no human being previously had to contend with. New prod-ucts. Lifestyle options. Sexual options. Marital and non-marital options. Divorce. Nonmonogamous relationships. Communal living. New authority figures. Career changes. Weakening of religious and family ties. Technological changes. Role reversals. Childrearing and even childbirth options. We have an opportunity overload.

One of my clients lamented recently, "How I wish that every morning someone would hand me my script, the script that told me what to choose. I'm so very tired of trying to figure, day in and day out, every decision on its own merit."

By applying the principles of centering, you will find an exciting, valid avenue to a more satisfying existence—one that will resolve the complexities that might surround you. There are six basic steps to the centering process: (1) choosing effective thoughts; (2) defining your inner self; (3) committing yourself to inner liberation; (4) attaining a full measure of calm; (5) clarifying purpose; and (6) enjoying adventure. The meaning of each of these will become progressively clearer to you as I take you, step by step, through this dynamic process. You will be shown, aided by real examples taken from my case files, exactly how you can apply these exciting principles immediately to your own life. The last chapter shows you how to continue to be inner-liberated permanently—regardless of how hectic your situation might become.

I want to emphasize that the inner-liberated way of life is not selfish. Nor is it a life that is marked by self-sacrifice and personal denial. In my view, selfishness should be tempered with the capacity for deep listening to and caring for others, while self-sacrifice and personal denial must be moderated by a healthy sense of self-care.

This book goes beyond the point where similar books often leave off. If you master only the first two steps (choosing your own thoughts and defining your inner self) you open up to yourself a choice of several new lifestyles. You can, for example, choose to become an irresponsible hedonist with a kind of playboy mentality. Hopefully, that is not all you want out of your life. Such a heady existence too often is destined to become an empty "trip to nowhere."

Another choice at that point is that of being the complete ascetic: one who watches life go by, an observer rather than a full participant. Attractive as this kind of life might seem at times, it is not at all what I have in mind. I am too curious about firsthand feelings. I want to experience life qualitatively, actively.

A personal note

The principles that I offer in this book have been derived from many years, in fact a lifetime, of searching, study, and self-discovery. However, the full realization of this way of life has only been mine for the past five years. Some of the best ideas, I realize, were inherited from family, certain friends, and a few exceptional teachers. Others were "gifts" I received from some of the students and clients with whom I've shared intimately through my professional practices as a teacher and therapist. And still other principles I discovered and sometimes rediscovered on my own —occasionally by the sheerest of accidents.

Although the basic ideas and principles of this book were undoubtedly fermenting within me for many years, it was one event in particular that jarred me sufficiently to realize fully this new and exciting way of life.

About five years ago, I was stumbling along in my mid-forties—a good job, active professionally, upwardly mobile, nice family, house in the suburbs, even a dog! Not too bad . . .

The dean of the college where I taught suddenly resigned. No sooner had I heard the news than the thought raced into my head, "My God, this is like a dream coming true. My big chance. I'll be the next dean. Why, I'm perfect for the job." Obviously, looking back now, I realize that I had always had a secret scenario, expecting to become very "important" in my field. "Who knows," I thought, "when I'll eventually become president of the college, chancellor —and Lord knows what next." I really thought that was my natural destiny.

Persons more realistic than I warned me that my candidacy might not flourish, but I refused to think even for a moment that I would not be successful.

As it turned out, not only was I unsuccessful, but I got practically no support whatsoever. I was at first—shocked! "How could they do this to me? After all, these are my friends. And didn't they all adore me?" I honestly had thought that most of them did. I fumed inside about the injustice of it all. My world fell apart. Dreams of grandeur turned to self-pity, self-pity to indignation, and indignation to anger. Anger at injustice (for me). Anger at the search committee. And especially anger at myself for being so angry. "What a hypocrite I am," I thought, "a therapist, and my own rage is driving me up the wall. And how can I expect to help others?" This anger, then self-pity, went on for months and months, with unpleasant and angry thoughts spinning around and around in my head. "This is no way to live," I thought. And then began a most fascinating process of internal self-change. Through centering, and in a surprisingly short period of time, an entire series of new, much more productive and enjoyable, thoughts filled my head. My life has taken a marvelous turn for the better, and I feel now that I have a style of personal existence that far exceeds anything that I would have previously dreamed possible.

Apparently this incident caught me just at the right time in my psychological development. No telling what the result might have been if this centering event had occurred when I was much younger. Undoubtedly, I would have become more "realistic" sooner—but I doubt that I would have had enough experience of life to have conceptualized an inner-liberated lifestyle for myself. In any case, the realization that I was not proceeding with my life in optimal fashion came through loud and clear to me. And over a period of just a few months, through some very effective activities and thoughts that I will describe quite fully, many truths that I had only half sensed previously seemed to fall most dramatically into place. I had found my center! I definitely became aware of who I am and what it is realistically that I want out of this life of mine. At this very moment I am proceeding with that plan, and I have every reason to believe that I will continue to progress in the future. I have ordered my priorities and feel totally realistic. The process that provided me with this position is the six-step centering process I describe in this book. "Inner-liberating" most aptly describes the kind of life I have been living these past five years, am currently enjoying, and expect to continue to enjoy in the time that I have remaining on this planet.

My life has taken on a deep and abiding sense of inner calm, something that I possessed very little of previously. In addition I have been living a life that has been filled with excitement and vitality. There has been plenty of life in my life. And with all of this I have enjoyed a pervasive sense of personal purpose and meaning. I would like to share my discoveries and methods with you.

Chapter
·2·
STEP ONE:
Choosing Effective Thoughts

*The last of human freedoms—to
choose one's attitude in any given
set of circumstances.*

—Dr. Viktor Frankl

There is no umbilical cord of any kind attaching you physically to any other person, place, or thing—at least there hasn't been since birth. You are, indeed, a separate entity. An individual. And because of this, you must fully appreciate this one very important factor, the most fundamental principle in this whole book. No one but you, ever, under any circumstances, chooses one of your thoughts for you. You and you alone do the choosing. There is no question that you have stored in your mind a countless number of conscious and less than conscious thoughts. And you alone can only pick one at a time to use.

The advantages that will accrue to you once you fully appreciate this powerful fact are enormous. However, let us consider the one disadvantage.

Once you begin taking full responsibility for choosing your own thoughts on a regular basis, you will no longer have the advantage of saying to yourself, "He, she, it, or they *made* me feel or act a certain way." If you have employed this generally overused defense, you are bound to miss it deeply. It is one of the most handy devices known to man and has prevented literally millions of people from taking responsibility for themselves. But, if you cling to this defense, you cannot expect to become inner-liberated.

The ultimate freedom. Dr. Viktor Frankl, an eminent psychiatrist, puts this principle this way: ". . . everything can be taken from a man, but one thing: the last of human freedoms—to choose one's attitude in any given set of circumstances, to choose one's own way." Frankl *chose* his own thoughts in order to survive the bestiality of Nazi concentration camps. But this powerful concept can be traced back for centuries, at least to the early Greek philosophers and probably as early as when man first began to think about thinking. For most of us this is not a new idea, but it is one that we have forgotten. This is unfortunate because it opens our lives to fantastic possibilities.

No thought is unthinkable. Once you learn to appreciate that it is you who choose your thoughts, one new freedom that instantly becomes yours is the freedom to choose whatever thoughts you want at any time. No thought is, in itself, unthinkable. You and I and everyone else have the capacity to think anything that we want to, any time we want to, and any place that we want to. You can choose thoughts that are beautiful, ugly, stimulating, dull, adventurous, friendly, fear-producing, crazy, absurd, logical, irrelevant, irreverent, dirty, tittilating, liberating, slanderous, peculiar, witty—anything at all and at any time at all. It's entirely up to you!

The Process of Thought Choice

Let us examine more precisely how this process of choosing of your own thoughts works. There is no way short of brain surgery by which anyone can get physically inside your head and *make* you choose a particular thought. They can try of course, and many persons certainly do. But the final *choice* of what it is that you think is totally yours. Another person can try in the most articulate manner possible to convince you to think a particular thought. But even the most articulate person in the world cannot force you to choose what he suggests or urges. Others, or outside circumstances, may influence what thoughts you choose, but in the final analysis the choice is always left to you. Accordingly, you have a tremendous amount of personal power reserved for you —but at the same time, you have an awesome responsibility for the way you choose to live your life.

YOUR THOUGHT STOREROOM

Picture your mind as a vast storeroom with many shelves. On the shelves are rows and rows of thoughts written on cardboard signs. They are stored systematically so the stockroom manager (you) can reach them whenever the occasion demands.

This storeroom is divided into a number of sections, each with thoughts for particular situations. The shelves easiest to reach are labeled "conscious thoughts." Thoughts that are rarely used are on the back shelves. The thoughts are placed in various categories: "intelligent thoughts," "counterproductive defective thoughts," and one category labeled "effective thoughts." (It is these effective thoughts that this book is about.) You also notice a number of shelves that are empty. Apparently these shelves await new thoughts that are bound to arrive from outside. Ah, but look. There are a number of shelves that have nothing but blank posters stored on them. These, you realize, are for creating thoughts of your own should a particular occasion call for such an original.

Suddenly there is an emergency! Someone outside is yelling at you. The thought light goes on; it says, "Send one thought up front, pronto, to contend with what that fellow is yelling." Now you really have a project on your hands.

What thought will *you choose?* This is difficult because you have literally millions of them in your files. Some of them were placed there many years ago at the suggestion of your parents, teachers, friends, and perhaps even an enemy or two. You check the shelves marked "Thoughts for Handling Epithets." You pass up choosing "Shut up you bastard," although, humanly enough, you give it a micromoment's consideration.

You are unable to find an effective thought for this occasion in your files, so you quickly decide to invent one just for this special situation. The thought you create is, "Ignore the epithet and pretend that you heard a compliment."

Your thought is translated into action as you speak your mind (as they say). Your senses bring back information that suggests your thought really did prove effective. And therefore, you place it caringly on your "Effectively Handling Epithets" shelf in case you need call on it again in the future.

You Can Control Your Feelings and Behavior by Thought Choice

Our lives are composed of a finite number of "present moments." During each of these moments you are busy choosing thoughts of one sort or another, consciously and unconsciously. Of course it would be unnecessary to pay attention to this natural process all the time even if you could. However, at those moments when you find that what you are experiencing is less than satisfying or that your behavior seems self-defeating, by paying more attention to your thought-choosing process you can select alternate thoughts, more effective thoughts, that permit you access to more productive ways of behaving. Is it not reassuring to know that when necessary you can learn to take charge of your feelings and behavior simply by selecting more effective thoughts?

THOUGHTS CREATE FEELINGS

It is well established in medicine that without a correlative thought you can have no feeling. It is the thought that you choose *after* nerve impulses are sent to your brain that suggests to you what is going on—what you should (or should not) feel. Your thought says, in a very real sense, "That's a feeling that you have going on there. Say, that feeling is painful. Ouch." Then you look down and notice that you've stepped on a thumbtack. However, without the thought there would be no such feeling at all. Anesthesiologists learned long ago how to block these nerve messages to the brain so that surgeons can operate on us when we are wide awake—under the influence of a local anesthetic.

Did you ever find yourself avoiding an automobile accident by instinctively turning the wheel or applying the breaks without a thought of fear at the moment that you took this instantaneous action? Then, perhaps many minutes after it was over, you got the shakes. Obviously, it was the *thoughts* you chose *after the fact* that created your emotional response—in this case fear, manifested by your shaking. And so it is with all of your feelings. No correlative thought, then no feeling. Without thoughts you would be little more than a vegetable. Therefore in order to feel good, it is necessary to concentrate on thought choice rather than feelings per se.

THOUGHTS CREATE BEHAVIOR

Your thoughts are also the key to the way you behave. You cannot possibly pick yourself up and walk from one spot to another and then sit down without the appropriate correlative thoughts. Did you ever see a chicken with its head cut off? Circles. Total aimlessness. The thought that sets your body in motion may take only an instant, but it is a thought nonetheless.

If you act nicely to someone, it is because you choose certain thoughts that enable you to act that way. You may have thought, "I like so and so, so I will be very kind." Or perhaps you chose thoughts that were a bit devious. "So and so has the power to do me a favor. I'll be very gracious to him." In any case, it is your thought choices that give rise to most of your behavior. Since thought choice is so powerful a factor in your life, it is well worth mastering.

Your thoughts are the master key to the doors of feelings and behavior. It is your feelings of course, which are most "real" to you, which enable you to feel "good," "indifferent," or "bad." It is within the realm of your feelings that you really live. Your behavior, on the other hand, as important as it is, is much like the tip of an iceberg, merely the part that goes public.

Do not be discouraged if you find yourself adamantly resisting taking responsibility for your thoughts. After all, it's more than likely that for most of your life you have been taught (and told time and time again, since it is deeply ingrained in popular folklore) that it was the external condition that *caused* you to think a certain way. You will have to fight the natural temptation to fall back on this convenient myth.

However, when you eventually develop the habit of saying, and more importantly of thinking, with conviction, "Neither she, he, they, nor it made me feel this way, but rather *I* have chosen thoughts that made me feel this way," you will be well along toward inner liberation. You must at first remind yourself at regular intervals (acknowledging but overcoming your natural resistances) that it is *you* who choose thoughts to create your feelings. Doing so will give you access to exciting new options in the way that you live your life.

A THOUGHT FOR YOUR FILES (choose one)

Defective Thought	Effective Thought
She hurt my feelings.	I chose thoughts that hurt my feelings.

I am not suggesting, of course, that you walk around reminding yourself all the time that you are choosing your own thoughts, feelings, and behavior. What I do recommend is that when you find yourself feeling or acting in ways that are proving unsatisfactory, you then remind yourself loudly and clearly that it is *you* who are *choosing* the thoughts that are making you feel or behave so disadvantageously. And of course that it is you who can choose other, more effective, more productive, thoughts if you really care to do so. As a result, you are left with little room to ever say that you've been "brainwashed." And although your dreams and fantasies may seem beyond your control at times, you must acknowledge that they take place inside your head. And if any person is to be in charge of these fantasies, it must be you and no one else.

Getting what you deserve

Here is a dramatization of an inner-liberated person's view of the advantages of self-responsibility.

Inner-liberated person: "I don't know if you've heard about it. I recently got a very big assignment, a terrific new job. A very big job. The biggest I have ever had."

Friend: "Marvelous. Good for you. What's it all about?"

"Well, you'll never believe this. This new assignment was just an offer that I couldn't refuse."

"Tell me about it. I'm very curious."

"I've just been appointed CHIEF EXECUTIVE!"

"Fantastic. Chief Executive in charge of what?"

"Chief Executive in charge of me. See, I told you it was a very

big job. It's undoubtedly the biggest job I've ever had in my entire life. I'm in charge, full charge, of a human being's life. That's some responsibility! It scares me a little. But let me tell you, I can't refuse the job. The pay is marvelous. I get paid exactly what I deserve. You can't ask for anything fairer than that. When I really do right by myself, I get rewarded accordingly. When I goof off, of course there's the proper deduction for that, too. After all, I don't expect something for nothing. I like this arrangement because I know that I'll do a good job. I'm a worker. This is the first job where the rewards are *perfectly* fair, and that's all I ever wanted—a fair shake."

Certainly this is an *effective* way of viewing the taking of responsibility for oneself, which brings us to the next point.

Defective Thoughts vs. Effective Thoughts

It is your counterproductive, self-defeating thoughts which account for most of your problems: problems at home, at work, in social situations. For example, you might want to blame that tediously slow driver in front of you, the one hogging the highway, for making you angry. But in reality he doesn't even know you. He probably doesn't even know you exist. No. The truth of the matter is that it is your thoughts, anger-producing thoughts, that are making you angry. And you choose and are totally responsible for your thoughts while you are driving. You are capable of choosing, at any time, in any place, all kinds of emotion-producing thoughts, joy-producing thoughts, even orgasm-producing thoughts. That attractive person across the room is not in any way *responsible* for the thoughts that you choose to think. It is your own thoughts that can "turn you on" or "turn you off." You have no boring meetings to attend at work. It is only you who will be to blame if you bring boring thoughts to the meeting. Simply prepare yourself in advance with interesting, portable, inconspicuous material that you can choose to think about if external things are of no significant value to you.

The full appreciation of the fact that nothing you ever choose to think at any time is "unthinkable" can free you to choose some highly imaginative and original thoughts. And why not? It's your mind and you can think anything that you want to with it! Why not choose the most effective thoughts possible?

SELF-VICTIMIZATION

Consider the problem of obesity, which so many Americans suffer from. There are millions of people who have moved unsuccessfully from one diet to another for most of their adult lives. Some experts, for instance, have suggested that certain unfortunate people have more fat cells than others and that these fat cells, more than anything else, compel these people to remain overweight. However, if you keep clearly in mind that you cannot get fat (under normal circumstances) without putting fattening foods in your own mouth and chewing and digesting them all by yourself, then you cannot comfortably blame fat cells, the delicious-looking cake, the dessert table, or anything else for what is most certainly a voluntary action on your part. After all, as adults no one has forced food into our mouths. It is our thoughts that victimize us if we overeat. But fortunately, we can learn how to control our thoughts and have them work in our behalf instead of against us. Naturally, this takes some practice.

A THOUGHT FOR YOUR FILES (choose one)

Defective Thought	Effective Thought
That attractive person over there is "turning me on." I can't help what I'm experiencing.	My thoughts about that person over there are "turning me on." Do I like what I'm experiencing?

Even the meaning of a word or two can make a tremendous difference in the way you think and consequently feel and act. The vocabulary that we use to do our thinking with is sometimes much too imprecise, and this imprecision can lead to serious misunderstandings in our conversation with ourselves. For example, take the well-worn maxim, "think positively." Positive thinking, if used too loosely, can lead to some treacherous, self-defeating errors in behavior.

Actually there are two types of positive thinking. The distinctions are extremely important. There is *realistic* positive thinking and *unrealistic* (Pollyanna-like) positive thinking, and misunderstanding this difference causes your errors in behavior.

By way of illustration, in the insurance business it is common practice to analyze how many calls are, on the average, necessary to produce one sale. Company records may show that a salesman can expect to make approximately one sale for every ten prospects seen. Now, supposing two different salesmen go out and approach their prospects, "thinking positively." Is it reasonable to assume that both men interpret "think positively" in the very same way? Of course not. Are you referring to realistic positive thinking or unrealistic (Pollyanna-like) positive thinking? The realistic positive-thinking salesman will make his ten calls and one sale, as will the unrealistic positive-thinking salesman. But the realistic positive-thinking salesman will have a much better time of it. He will approach his day's work with this attitude: "I'll make my ten calls, give ten good sales' pitches, possibly be rejected nine times and probably make one sale." However, the Pollyanna salesman will have a much more brutal day. He will think like this: "I'm going to make a sale every time I give a pitch. Think positive, think positive." He is bound to be rejected nine times out of ten, the same as his coworker. But at each rejection he will be jolted. Consequently, he will be mighty exhausted. Positive thinking is far too vague a term to be used as indiscriminately as it usually is.

Therefore, I will sometimes go to exceptional lengths in this book to point out the difference between such concepts as right thoughts and effective thoughts (there are subtle differences and major consequences for the user if the differences are not clear). There are also differences between "due concern" and "worry" and, as you will shortly see, major differences between "inner liberation" and the conventional meanings and usages of such concepts as "openness," "spontaneity," and "sensuality."

A THOUGHT FOR YOUR FILES (choose one)

Defective Thought	Effective Thought
I'm a positive thinker. I look on the bright side—always.	I'm a realistic positive thinker. I face the facts as is—and work upward from there.

NOT A MATTER OF RIGHT OR WRONG

An effective thought is a productive thought that works on your behalf. Since you are free to choose any thought that you like, choosing an *effective* thought can serve you in much better fashion than simply choosing a so-called "right" thought. For the inner-liberated person, there is no such thing as right-thinking people and wrong-thinking people. Instead, he tends to look at thoughts in terms of whether they are effective or ineffective, or productive or counterproductive.

Dana, a thirty-three-year-old former client on the verge of divorce, was caught up and victimized by his "right" thinking. He complained about his wife, Tracy. "She doesn't take the garbage out of the kitchen for hours and hours. She just lets it sit there. Sometimes it just sits there five or six hours after dinner. It's just not right. My mother never did that. Mother got the garbage out of the house right away—immediately. Who wants garbage sitting around the house? Not me, certainly."

"Dana," I said, "have you been able to convince your wife to look at it your way?"

"Well, I tried. But Tracy doesn't seem to listen. We've had long conversations; somehow I don't seem to be able to communicate."

"Then why don't you change your own opinion? After all, at least you can manage your own opinion, your own thoughts. You can't expect to be responsible for hers."

Dana was able, through concentration, to choose not to let the garbage issue unnerve him. He had two "effective" options: to choose thoughts that permitted him to live with the garbage in the house for six hours or so, or to take the garbage out himself. Dana chose the first option.

In this case, neither Dana nor his wife was "right." The garbage of the average American household is rarely garbage in the eyes of many other parts of the world. Household garbage is primarily an attitude or opinion. And certainly there are no logical reasons why this family's excess should be removed immediately—five or six hours was not enough time for decomposition to take place. Since Dana finally realized that he could not do anything to make his wife change, he simply permitted himself to change by choosing effective thoughts. He stopped clinging protectively, defensively (and certainly ineffectively, in view of the circumstances) to "right" thoughts. Many a relationship has been destroyed because one party felt convinced that he was "right" when right or wrong had no genuine bearing on the problem.

Another couple, Ben and Vera, who had been married for twenty-seven years, unhappily for the most part, were attempting to improve their relationship through counseling. However, about six months after they had prematurely terminated counseling, Ben wrote me a letter. He asked me to put in writing who was "right." "Vera keeps saying that you told her that I was wrong. I told her that I distinctly heard you say our problems were because of her attitude toward her mother." I reminded Ben that it was hardly an issue of right or wrong and that rather, both parties played a part. It was the *system* that had defects in need of repair, not necessarily one party being right or wrong. It is important to remind yourself periodically that you have the responsibility to choose effective thoughts that work in your behalf rather than so-called right thoughts.

A THOUGHT FOR YOUR FILES (CHOOSE ONE)

Defective Thought	Effective Thought
I'm not really responsible for myself. Outside circumstances *make* me act certain ways.	The one thing that I truly own is me. I accept and enjoy full responsibility for myself. I keep my eye on myself without being self-conscious. I've noticed that wherever I go, there I am.

Here's a personal example, an example of how an effective thought choice was used to help change my feelings.

One evening recently, I was driving to upstate New York to give a lecture. "Whew, am I tired," I thought to myself, as I stared bleary-eyed over the steering wheel. I could hardly manage to keep my eyes open, yet I knew that within the next half hour I would be facing a large audience of professionals. Besides, driving while feeling so tired is dangerous. Then I reminded myself that I wasn't really tired, but rather it was my thoughts that were making me tired. This didn't ring true to me at first. "Who are you kidding? I'm really tired. I have every right to be tired. Up late last night. Working hard." The whole routine. But then the wiser part of myself persisted. "No, it's your thoughts that are making you tired. You know that's the case. Now's the time to put what you know, what you preach, into practice." I then said to myself, rather dryly at first, "You're choosing thoughts that are making you tired. That's right, tired thoughts." I allowed that admission to penetrate the defenses that are so often mounted against taking personal responsibility for one's own thoughts and feelings. It took a few moments, but the reality of what I was saying to myself eventually penetrated. I then began to think wake-up thoughts, unthinkable, mischievous, devious thoughts. These thoughts definitely aroused me. Aroused me, perhaps, a little too much. In any case, I arrived at the lecture hall full of pep and energy. Why not be energetic and *effective*, instead of deservedly tired and *ineffective?*

A THOUGHT FOR FILES (CHOOSE ONE)

Defective Thought	Effective Thought
Things in this world really make me nervous. I have a perfect right to be nervous considering the circumstances.	If I ever get nervous, I say, "You're making yourself nervous." Then I say, "Are you enjoying or valuing being nervous?" Then I usually answer, "No, I am not enjoying being nervous." So then I say, "Stop choosing thoughts that make you nervous and start choosing thoughts that make you calm." Then I follow my instructions to the letter and end up very calm.

Mindset—The Way You Look at Things

The principle of "set" has been well established in experimental psychology. All of us, in one way or another, have been preconditioned to look at many things (or situations) from a particular point of view. It is this point of view, or mindset, that colors much of our thinking. We are, in a real sense, "programmed" to think in a particular way. Here are a few examples, some of which might be familiar to you. (Check for the correct answers at the end of this list of examples.)

Example 1: What is this?

Example 2: A doctor and his son are involved in a serious car accident. The son is badly injured, and the doctor is killed. The boy is rushed to the emergency room of the hospital. The surgeon, taking one look at the boy, turns away and says, "I cannot help this boy. He is my son." How is this possible?

Example 3: Is the capital of Kentucky pronounced Louis—ville or Louey—ville?

Example 4: Of what is this a picture?

Answers:
(1) This is an aerial view of a Mexican riding a bicycle.
(2) The doctor was a woman.
(3) Neither. The capital of Kentucky is Frankfort.
(4) This could be either a goblet or a mirror image of a man's profile—depending on how you look at it, whether you look at the negative space (the outside) or the positive space. (Looking at all kinds of things with an eye toward the negative and positive space can literally double the quality of your perceptual experiences.)

There are numerous other examples of this type, many of which you might have learned as a child. As youngsters, most of us enjoyed these kinds of things as puzzles and jokes. But behind all of them is a very powerful principle that can be gainfully employed. The principle of set, once fully appreciated, can be used *for* us—quite easily. If a set acts to our advantage, we keep it, if not, we drop it and change to another.

BREAKING SET

Just as you broke set with the above examples and are now fully aware of how another perspective makes things clearer, you can break set just as easily on any other occasion that suits you. Breaking set in day-to-day activities simply means that you back off from your programmed view and take a new stance. Once you do that, you will not be inclined to fall back in the same trap again.

Some time ago a very interesting experiment was performed regarding mindset. An actor who was an expert at double-talk was hired to be the guest speaker at a convention of medical doctors, certainly a highly educated group. The actor was introduced by their chairman as an expert in a very specialized and complex branch of medicine. He proceeded to give a forceful and articulate talk on his "very complex specialty." But unbeknownst to the audience, he was only talking double-talk, masterly perhaps, but double-talk nonetheless. When the audience was asked to rate the talk afterward, they rated it as excellent in terms of delivery and superior when it came to the speaker's knowledge of subject matter.

The frightening thing about all of this is that even well-trained and sophisticated physicians were so easily victimized by their mindset—the fact that the actor was introduced by their chairman (someone whom they apparently trusted) as a qualified expert. So many of us can be readily duped by form over substance if we are not careful.

Naturally, we cannot be on guard all the time. But we should also be aware that it is our conditioning that sets us up toward a particular view rather than the object itself that we are viewing. There are a number of different ways of looking at almost anything, so why not look at everything in such a way that it will do you the most good?

A number of years ago I was participating in a training workshop for counselor educators. As part of the workshop, one of the leaders created (set up) an interesting exercise involving several teams of five persons each. The task of each team, the workshop leader explained, was to assemble a jigsaw puzzle of about twenty separate pieces. The team that completed the puzzle first would win the contest. There was, however, to be one special rule that would make cooperation very difficult: we were not to speak or make sounds of any kind in order to communicate with our teammates.

On a given signal we all started, and I became a very active and highly motivated participant in this activity. My team was working well together in spite of the handicap of not talking. After about seven or eight hard-working minutes, we seemed to be about halfway done. I looked over to see how our competition was doing. Much to my dismay, I noticed that one of the teams was almost done, and to my shock and annoyance, I noticed that several of their members were whispering to each other. *Whispering,* I had distinctly heard our leader say, *was absolutely against the rules.* They had audaciously violated the rules!

Naturally, this disobedient team won. They didn't have the handicap that the rest of us were saddled with, and the leader did not see fit to penalize them—even though what they were doing was obvious to almost everyone. For a while I was deeply annoyed and irritated. It was then that I broke set. A new perspective suddenly dawned on me, perhaps in the same way that you realized that Frankfort was the capital of Kentucky.

Who was it that said we must not talk? Was that an order directly from the Gospel? Of course not. It was just the instruction of a human being (just like me); his instructions were not laws from the Almighty, and for the first time in my life I fully appreciated that I had a choice even when given specific instructions and rules. Previous to that point, I had followed orders from above blindly. That can be extremely dangerous, regardless of how well-meaning or benign the role-playing leader is. I have come to realize that all leaders are "role-playing." It remains up to me, in each and every case, to decide independently whether or not I want to play his game by his rules. Of course, if I choose to break the rules, I must be prepared to face the consequences. This applies in real life to such role-playing leaders as college presidents, chairmen, deans, or anyone in a power role over me for that matter.

A THOUGHT FOR YOUR FILES (CHOOSE ONE)

Defective Thought	Effective Thought
The rules have been stated clearly by my boss. I have no choice but to follow them. After all, she's the boss. An order is an order.	The rules have been stated clearly by the person *acting* as boss. I reserve the right to choose whether I wish to abide by them. After all, she might be fallible. Let me think for a moment and decide if I'm willing to go along with her directions.

Of course, I fully realize that if I disobey the authority, there is likely a price to pay—and I'm wise enough to be prepared for that. But no matter what the price, it is still up to me to decide, each and every time, whether I choose to play follow-the-leader or not.

I am not suggesting that you endlessly question all authority. Obviously, there are times and occasions when even to pause for a moment and question might cause an unnecessary hardship, even the loss of a life. But this questioning is usually inappropriate only during emergencies— life and death situations. Most other times, it is not only permissible, it is wise. I have found out since I have had this new mindset that I have had more freedom than I ever thought was possible. The fact is that I rarely exercise this freedom, but as I'm sure you can appreciate, it is most delightful for me to know that I possess it.

Who says that I can't just get up and leave the theater in the middle of a play? That I have to be at work on time? That I have to act a certain way toward others? The answer is—no one but me.

What about being at work on time? Do I really have a choice? The answer is, yes, I do have a choice. "But if you're late too often, you might very well be fired." And my response to that is, "Yes, but it is still up to me to decide if I want to be late or not. I will probably have some leeway before the boss fires me—but if it were to come to that, well, I'd be prepared to handle it." What you will see shortly is that an inner-liberated attitude will prepare you for almost all the contingencies that life has to offer. An "I can handle it" attitude will develop. The truth is that I am hardly ever late for work, it's just not my style. But believe me, it is reassuring to know that I have all that freedom of choice—provided, of course, that I am prepared to handle the flack should it come, as it probably will.

Preparing in advance to handle the flack should it come is the key to this entire attitude. Surprisingly, as you will see shortly, there is very little in life that you really will not be able to handle once you know how to choose the necessary effective thoughts.

A THOUGHT FOR YOUR FILES (CHOOSE ONE)

Defective Thought	Effective Thought
That bastard will someday get punished by the fates. I don't know what it will be, but justice will triumph.	That guy won't necessarily "get his." This may not be the way I wish the world worked, but it often does operate that way. Justice doesn't always triumph. I've learned to live with that and not use up much of my limited time eating my heart out waiting for justice.

THINKING TWICE

Dr. Stanley Milgram performed an experiment to examine the extent to which people are blindly obedient to authority. Having hired a number of assistants for a professional experiment in which the subjects were to be given increasingly heavy doses of electric shocks if they were not performing correctly, he placed them under his supervision. The subjects (who were really actors in the employ of Milgram) pretended convincingly that they were experiencing inhuman amounts of pain. "Go on, administer greater voltage," Milgram ordered. He found that a very high percentage (over 60 percent) of people will listen to authority indiscriminately, even when it comes to inflicting harm on other human beings. And, of course, Nazi Germany is a clear example of how many "normal" people can be influenced to follow the dictates of an authoritarian leader.

Thinking twice about accepting the orders (suggestions) of any leader, supposedly good or not so good, is a good idea. Naturally, people who think this independently are not easily managed (or manipulated). Things might not be all that orderly and neat if the vast majority of people become this autonomous. However, the interest, variety, and excitement of a pluralistic society would certainly more than compensate for any disorderliness. And certainly, no dictator could hope to flourish in the midst of such independent individuals.

In order to break set and gain a new perspective, time and distance certainly help. That is why those, for example, who have lost a loved one can, after a reasonable period of time and under normal circumstances, find another love to help replace the one they lost. But time alone does not heal. A new set must ensue.

This takes some distancing. Looking at the situation from another angle, Marshall McLuhan, the Canadian philosopher, pointed out that an ant in an anthole does not know where it is until it leaves the anthole and views it from the top and on the outside. Only then can it see the hole from a distance, from a different perspective. Only then can the ant say with confidence, "Oh, look where I've been." That's why an American can only see that Americans tend to walk differently when he returns home from overseas, or that our cars and roads are so much larger than those elsewhere. He has both a new sense of perspective and a sense of compassion.

NEUTRALIZING DEFECTIVE THOUGHTS

Morris was asked to give a talk about a trip he took to the Middle East. He really prepared himself well this time because he knew from past experience that if it wasn't solidly prepared, he had a tendency to get very nervous in front of an audience and freeze up. This time he promised himself that he would not panic. He said to himself, over and over, "Morris, be calm. Morris, be calm." And suddenly there he was in front of the group, about to utter his first words. He looked out over the sea of faces, and then he heard that little demon voice inside of his head. "Morris, this is terrible. They're all looking at you. You're in a panic! You can't talk without reading your notes." "Go away," Morris said to the demon voice, but it would not go away. So Morris, with a dry mouth and a nervous, trembling voice, was forced once again to read his entire "talk" from his note cards without so much as looking up even once. Morris's subconscious had failed him—once again. The problem here, clearly, is to put those overactive, self-defeating defective thoughts in their place once and for all.

In a very genuine sense we have all been "hypnotized" to believe certain things about ourselves—some good things and some not so good. Perhaps someone laughed at you when you were a child and a few defective thoughts entered your subconscious—"I'm ugly," or "I'm foolish." Or, perhaps you interpreted this laughter in a more productive fashion. "I'm witty," or "I'm fun." If you have effective thoughts in your subconscious, enjoy and keep them. If you have some that are defective, you must neutralize them. Here are some examples of effective and defective thoughts:

Effective Thoughts

I'm prone to do well in whatever I try.
I tend to finish whatever I start, if I really want to.
I'm quite lovable.
I'm effectively loving.
I'm graceful.
I'm effectively open.
I'm not a fearful or nervous person.

Defective Thoughts

I'm lazy.
I'm not able to draw a straight line (dance, sing, whistle, etc.).
I'm guilt ridden.
I'm stupid.
I can't stop thinking about so and so.
I'm a worrier.
I'm afraid to take chances.
I'm ugly and unlovable.
I'm such a bad person to be around.

Sometimes those overactive, counterproductive thoughts that lie in your subconscious actually leap forward in order to be chosen by you when you are in the process of making a thought selection. It is important to recognize that you can have only *one* thought in the *foreground* of your mind in a given instant. When that thought recedes into the background, it is only then that another thought is permitted to take its place—centerstage. All of the thoughts that we allow out on centerstage were chosen only by us—even the defective ones.

Three Plans for Overcoming Defective Thoughts

There are three plans that can help you overcome counterproductive thoughts: Plan A is the conscious approach that we've been exploring (and that most of this book is about);

Plan B is the subconscious approach, your next alternative; and Plan C is the deepest (and generally expensive) and longest route. It requires an expert professional helper, trained in counseling and psychotherapy.

In most instances, Plan A, which consists of deliberately choosing effective thoughts and avoiding defective thoughts, does the job. In essence, (when you can't sleep, for example) you are saying to yourself, "Go away, stupid thought ('I can't sleep.'), and take over, effective thought ('I'm peaceful, ready for rest. I'm about to fall asleep.')."

Your second option, Plan B, provides a means for a more decisive reprogramming of your subconscious, where the defective thoughts reside. It involves autosuggestion, a kind of harmless, easy-to-do self-hypnosis. As you become familiar with Plan B, you will find that it takes very little time and will prove extremely effective in your dealing with any unwanted thought.

As a last resort, you might have to rely on Plan C to quiet unwanted thought, but only in those unusual instances when Plans A and B have proved themselves inadequate for the task.

Plan C, psychotherapy, although not the subject of this book, can often be a useful adjunct to the centering principles that we are discussing. But even with the help of an excellent therapist, you will ultimately still be left with the responsibility of choosing your own effective thoughts—and ridding yourself of counterproductive thoughts completely on your own. No one can live your life for you, and in reality the only genuine, lasting help will be self-help.

PLAN A: DEALING WITH A "RUNAWAY" FEELING

Sometime or another you might feel that an emotion is running away with you, and you find that fighting it directly proves useless. For example, did you ever feel depressed, but for no clear reason? Then did you try to pep yourself up and find that the more you tried to feel better, the worse you began to feel?

You can usually lift your "downer" feelings by not trying so hard. That is, you merely apply a very powerful method called the go-along technique, a technique I informally refer to as the John Wayne technique.

Picture in your mind John Wayne in one of those old-time cowboy movies. He is, of course, riding a beautiful stallion and wearing a big white hat. The little lady from back East is bouncing wildly along in her horse and wagon, which has gone totally out of control. The fair maiden screams for help and there's John Wayne to the rescue on his stallion! Wayne brings his mount alongside the wagon and leaps bravely from his horse onto the buckboard. The horse and wagon are obviously far out of control, but big John does not falter. He crawls to the front of the wagon, climbs over the wild horses, and grasps the reins. Mr. Wayne, now fully asserting control, does not stop but rides the horse and buggy *another* mile or so down the road, affirming that he is in control of the wild horses. The horses begin to sense that someone is holding the reins—and they slow down. After a short period of time, he looks over to the admiring maiden and says, "Whooah," to the horses, bringing them to a full stop. The maiden smiles apprecia-tively as Big John turns the now docile horses and heads off in another direction, the direction of his choice. The back-ground music becomes gentle as Big John and the fair easterner ride off into the sunset.

Our hero offers an important lesson here. Imagine that your thoughts are running wild in a particular mindset, as did the horse-drawn waggon. (Your thoughts might run wild into depression, disenchantment, anger, fear, any number of counterproductive directions.) John Wayne did something very intelligent and natural in this little scenario that we rarely choose to do when we are trying to catch a runaway series of thoughts. He went along with what was already going on. Then, when eventually he found the reins of the wild horses, he rode with them *in the direction that they were going* for a short time. He asserted to them that he was in charge—even though they were off and running. It became impossible for the poor horses to sense whether they were still in command or John Wayne was. Mr. Wayne made certain that the horses knew that it was he who held the reins. After he sensed that they were fully aware that he was in charge, he pulled them to a halt. Only then did he turn them in the direction that he wished to go—off into the sunset. Once you have shown your runaway thoughts that it is you who are in charge of them, it is within your power to take your thoughts and feelings where you choose.

A fifty-two-year-old widow, Olga, a friend of mine, told me how angry her twenty-one-year-old daughter, Ann, made her feel. Olga had raised her daughter on her own (her husband died when their daughter was only three) and with great personal sacrifice. Working overtime countless hours as a typist, she saw to it that Ann could afford to go on to college. Then in her junior year, Ann, without the slightest consultation with her mother, quit school and ran off "to live with a dreadful, unemployed musician," as Olga put it. "I have a perfect right to be angry, don't I?" she asked, seeking reassurance. "After all that I've sacrificed, look how little I have to show for it."

Olga told me how she learned to take personal responsibility for her plight and eventually, to turn her unhappy situation around.

Although she continued to believe that her daughter's behavior was abominable and unjust, she managed to come to grips with the reality that there was absolutely nothing she could do about her daughter's behavior, at least at this time. She saw that there was nothing to be gained by remaining in her present state of anger. Here is how Olga proceeded to link up with her anger-producing thoughts, take full command, and turn to a more productive kind of thinking.

When she first realized how angry she was, she acknowledged the fact, "Wow, am I angry. I'm not just angry—I'm
furious." Then she said (in her mind's eye, of course), "I'm
choosing these thoughts that are making me angry." These
words almost stuck in her throat. It was difficult, naturally,
for Olga to admit that it was her thoughts and not her
daughter's behavior that made her feel so angry. After all,
she had more than fifty years of previous conditioning and
training in blaming outside conditions for what she was
feeling inside. However, she eventually did manage to link
up with her anger-producing mindset. Then she carried her
anger as far as she wanted to. "Let's see," she thought, "let
me try to make my stomach get tight." That thought
helped, and her stomach got a bit tighter than it already
was. Then she tried to think a thought or two that would
make her clench her fists more and tighten up her jaw.
Again she met with some success, demonstrating to her
previously out-of-control anger-producing thoughts that
she was firmly in control. After a while she had had enough
of anger and decided to think thoughts that would make
her calm. She chose some thoughts about yellow flowers in
a beautiful green field that she had stored in her memory.
Slowly, her pulse returned to normal. The flow of angry
adrenaline came to a stop. Olga took off, in her mind's eye,
into the sunset, past the yellow flowers, and over the beautiful green hill. Olga had successfully linked up with her
undesirable thoughts; she took command and turned her
emotional state completely around. Of course, she still had
a lot of unresolved business with her daughter—but that
she was able to "work-through" later at her own pace.

One might ask, "Isn't such control a form of repression?
Won't that anger come out somewhere else? Won't Olga,
for example, find it necessary to kick the dog when she gets
home—just to let this buried anger out?" But, the answer
to this query is a resounding no. This is not repression at
all. Olga fully acknowledged her angry thoughts. She did
not repress her anger. She rode with this emotion for a

while, took command of the feeling, took responsibility for the thoughts that were producing the feeling, and simply chose other, more effective, thoughts—which produced more effective (less angry) feelings.

Still, you might be wondering, what about when Olga's mind drifts back to thoughts of her daughter living with that musician that she despises? Won't those thoughts make her just as angry as before? After all, her daughter was not very sensitive to her mother's feelings or respectful of her mother's wishes. And Olga did apparently sacrifice a great deal for her daughter's college education, did she not?

Of course, I agree that if Olga returns to thinking about herself as self-sacrificing or betrayed, she is bound to get angry. However, over a period of time, she developed more effective (and much more realistic) attitudes toward her daughter's dropping out of college and living with someone without being married, which were but a few ideas that were upsetting to her. There are, of course, a variety of ways of looking at many of the issues that life presents. For example, who ever said, "Count on your children to respect you"? That may be nice, but it is not an inner-liberating concept, as you will come to see.

The point is that if one does not choose the thoughts that produce anger or any other emotion, then such an emotion does not come into being. Therefore no emotion is being repressed. So then by choosing your thoughts intelligently, you can greatly reduce, if not eliminate, any unwanted emotional condition, be it fear, worry, guilt, tension, etc.

Sometimes, it is difficult to deal with a feeling when you are unable to identify the particular thoughts causing such a feeling. A few years ago, Rose, the meticulously groomed thirty-three-year-old wife of a successful surgeon, came to me for counseling, complaining of a generalized feeling of anxiety. "I get very depressed all of a sudden, and I don't seem to be able to put my finger on just why. I get this horrible low feeling that just comes on me out of the blue, and I don't know what to do about it. It seems to come for no apparent reason, even when everything in my life is going well. I have almost everything I always wanted. Materially, we're blessed. My husband is loving and caring. Our children are terrific. Why do I get this way? What can I do about it?"

My recommendation to her was identical to that which we have been discussing. In essence: "Go along with the feeling for a while. Don't try so hard to fight it—or to figure out what's causing it. Choose thoughts that will make you even more depressed. Make yourself sad by thinking of all the things others have that you don't have. Make yourself cry a little because you are not appreciated by everyone. Identify in yourself something that can make you feel down, and then choose thoughts that will bring you down even further. By doing this, you will be taking charge of your feelings. Then, after a reasonable period of time—the shorter the better— ask yourself, 'Is this the way I want to continue to feel?' And then if your answer is no, choose thoughts that take you into a different emotional state. It's easier done than said, so start taking charge of your feeling states now."

What seemed to be adding to Rose's anxiety was the fear that she was out of control. By going along with and then deepening her depression, she enabled herself to get a handle on what was at first out of her reach.

Sometimes, of course, because of years of family conditioning, some people do learn to *repress* their emotions— leading to a wooden existence. In those instances it becomes necessary to permit oneself to feel more deeply— even such emotions as anger or hate can be valuable.

Foster and Elaine, a couple having marital difficulties, came to me for counseling. Elaine's complaint centered on Foster's "lack of emotion, lack of being able to express feelings." "He's so damn nice about everything that it makes me sick. I only wish that he would get angry once in a while. But no. All he ever does is smile and be nice. I can't stand it anymore."

Foster wanted to be more expressive, he said; "But what

can I do about it?" Eventually he figured out that he, alone, would have to take responsibility, for his lack of emotional expression. By choosing thoughts, quite deliberately, to make himself angry and by also choosing thoughts that said, "It's okay to express such feelings sometimes; it might even help my relationship with Elaine," Foster learned to become more expressive.

Going along with and then taking charge of any undesired emotion is an extremely effective tool that you must remind yourself to employ. Moreover, you must remind yourself that even though life might sometimes treat you unfairly there is still much that you can do to at least lessen the damage. Which brings us to the next powerful concept.

With Plan A, you consciously choose effective thoughts, employing the John Wayne tactic when needed. This suffices for most counterproductive thoughts. But if such a thought remains troublesome, even after using Plan A, you can then turn to Plan B, Autosuggestion, which reaches a little deeper, below the surface.

PLAN B: AUTOSUGGESTION

Your subconscious is composed of thoughts that are stored in your mind at a less than conscious (subconscious) level. A neurosurgeon, Dr. W. Penfield, reported in 1959 that, through electrical stimulation of the brain, one of his patients was enabled to recall vividly images that he had long since forgotten at a conscious level. Your brain has not forgotten a single thing that you have ever perceived. When you act at an "intuitive" level, you are really relying on these less than conscious memories (thoughts) that you have stored in your mind. Some of these thoughts lie dormant and harmless. Others are overactive—some quite productive and others counterproductive. It is the defective, overactive, less than conscious thoughts that we can neutralize by autosuggestion.

Autosuggestion has been misunderstood because it has been so abusively handled by charlatans and stage hypnotists for so many years. No one need be made to feel foolish or embarrassed by using this technique—there is absolutely nothing magical or secret about it. I deliberately avoid using the misnomer hypnosis as much as possible, because the prefix *hypno* is derived from the Greek word that means sleep. But you are never really asleep when you employ this technique. Rather, you are preoccupied with your imagination—you are entranced! Actually, it is more like the condition you are in just before you fall asleep each night.

Undoubtedly, you have been entranced on many occasions: while driving past your freeway exit, watching a good movie, reading an interesting book, staring at the TV, or even sitting in a classroom. Your power of imagination, your capacity for creative self-deception, and the ability to make suggestions to yourself are all fully utilized when you engage in the technique of autosuggestion.

Through the autosuggestion technique (Plan B), you are able to rest your conscious mind and speak directly to your subconscious. All that is involved is that you "reprogram" your subconscious and tell it in no uncertain terms to, in essence, "keep that dumb defective thought that keeps cropping up quiet."

Tricks for your imagination

Imagination is the process whereby you actually see an image or picture in your mind's eye without necessarily having the stimulus for the image in your actual physical vicinity. Interestingly, if you imagine something happening vividly enough, your body and nervous system will react just as if that which you are imagining is actually taking place. It is surprising how easy it is to trick your whole body and entire nervous system by using the powers of imagination. For example, if you were to imagine that a shadow behind a curtain is really the figure of an intruder, your hand might actually begin to sweat, your mouth get dry, your heart rate quicken. A person's body and nervous system reacts in exactly the same way whether it is really an intruder, a friend, disguised as an intruder, playing a poor practical joke, or merely a shadow from the tree outside.

It is not that our nervous systems and bodies are stupid. It is merely that figuring out whether our thoughts are right or wrong is not the job of our nerves and body. That is the job of our mind. Consequently, our imagination can be employed as either a very good friend or a very poor one. Why not, then, make your own imagination a very good friend?

You must use your imagination to "get past" your conscious mind and speak directly to your subconscious. Your conscious mind is much more orderly and logical than your subconscious mind. The former is usually skeptical about outside suggestions, and skepticism is generally a pretty good idea. But in order to reprogram your subconscious mind, you must get past this cautious gatekeeper. This is where the use of creative temporary self-deception comes into play.

Here is how you employ creative self-deception. Put the conscious, logical, skeptical part of your mind to rest. That is, gain your conscious mind's confidence, and then surreptitiously slip the effective new thought (that you've planned in advance) past it while it is looking the other way. Treat your subconscious mind to more effective new thoughts regularly in this manner. A person's subconscious is extremely trusting and naive. That's why the conscious part of you is so protective. Once something gets past the conscious gatekeeper, the subconscious gobbles up, quite indiscriminately, this new data. In this instance, of course, you are going to feed only thoughts that are very effective. It is difficult, if not impossible, to tell what has slipped into your subconscious over your lifetime. But that matters little once you have in your hands an effective means to reprogram yourself properly.

A simple procedure

(You will find a complete autosuggestion script in the Appendix on page 231 that can be used any time you wish to neutralize defective thoughts.)

Autosuggestion is a three-stage procedure. Stage 1: Place yourself in a very relaxed, trancelike state. Stage 2: Convince your relaxed conscious mind to trust the suggestions that you are about to offer. Create a set where that normally judgmental mind of yours suspends its critical judgment for a while, a form of creative self-deception. Stage 3: Speak directly to your subconscious and inject into it the effective thoughts that you have prepared in advance. Then, simply tell yourself to return to a fully conscious state—rested and relaxed—by counting slowly from one to five. And that's it.

Through this process you will have planted the new effective thought that can counter the defective thought. Now you can fully expect that your subconscious will work for you in a given instance rather than against you. Use this method to prepare yourself in advance any time you have to take a risk or undertake a new challenge. Autosuggestion is a safe technique, long known, fully researched—and it really works. Let's go over the three stages once again, with a little more detail.

Stage 1: Relaxing your conscious, critical mind. This is achieved merely by progressively suggesting to your body and mind that they relax. Take yourself to as quiet a place as you can conveniently find, then talk yourself down. This is a form of meditation. You suggest pictures to yourself that are soothing and comforting. In the appendix, on page 000, you will find a script that you can tape-record if you like. It will put you in a very relaxed state.

Stage 2: Bypassing your critical, conscious mind by gaining its confidence (creative self-deception). At this point, all you have to do is create a set in your conscious mind, which suggests to it that it has nothing to worry about, that it can trust you and your suggestions. Of course, you will do nothing to hurt either it or you. Say to your conscious self, in effect, "Trust me. Now you will not be able to open your eyes, conscious mind, even if you try." Okay, now try to open your eyes. No matter how hard you try, you will not be able to. Of course, your conscious mind, if it really wanted to, could open your eyes, but you have gained its confidence. It goes along with your figuring that you are a decent enough person and mean no harm. Once it does and finds that no harm has come to it, it relaxes its guard even more and trusts you implicitly. A set of trust is established.

Stage 3: Reprogramming your subconscious with effective thoughts. Now you are ready to tell your subconscious, "I will be very confident when I get up to make that speech tomorrow," or "I will finish that project that I started," or some other very productive suggestion. Or, perhaps, you might just quell an unwanted thought by telling it to keep quiet and get some rest. In this way, you have programmed your subconscious. It will really work in your behalf now, as it was most certainly meant to. Then simply suggest to yourself that by counting to five you will return to consciousness, fully refreshed and relaxed.

Use autosuggestion regularly

It is useful to program your intuition to work for you in advance of difficult situations. Preparing yourself in advance through autosuggestion, to enjoy your day, your work, even some of the difficult people you must deal with is a productive habit. You can use Plan B to help you sleep better, be on time, get down to business, or even to enjoy playing more.

Best of all, the more you use it, the easier it becomes to use.

PLAN C: PSYCHOTHERAPY AND COUNSELING

Plan C is your third option and need be resorted to only on those unusual occasions when Plans A and B have proved insufficient. Professional counseling and psychotherapy require the intervention and help of a trained person. It is an effective but generally a very costly and time-consuming approach. Sometimes a therapist, given sufficient training and knowledge, can act as a support as you go about implementing Plans A and B on your own. You should understand that there are innumerable approaches used in therapy, some bordering on the outlandish. The most important question you should find an answer to before you put yourself in the hands of an "expert" is, "Does he have his own house in order?"

OCCASIONAL INJUSTICES

It is one of the unavoidable facts of life that each of us now and then, perhaps some more than others, gets mistreated, treated unfairly, or, put in less gentle terms, "gets screwed." This is just one of the natural hazards of living in society, a basic penalty.

Sometimes we catch a cold when someone else, who deserves it more, doesn't. Sometimes our car breaks down in the middle of the highway, even though our mechanic just checked it out, said it was perfect, and charged us forty dollars for his appraisal. Sometimes a colleague at work who has been ducking responsibility gets more praise than you do. Or your spouse might accuse you of extravagance when you've really denied yourself some luxuries. Or your child might tell you to drop dead—and after all you've done for him! Life, as you must know, can sometimes be extremely unfair.

Justice is such an abstract and relative concept that inner-liberated persons have learned how to stop eating their hearts out about the times they don't seem to get a fair shake. In one large global sweep, they have *mourned in advance* for the fact that they are likely to be treated quite unfairly from time to time. They might even cry. Their hearts ache for themselves. It's part of their recognition that, fundamentally, they are unique and sometimes quite alone in this world. They wish they could always be fully appreciated, that they could always get a fair shake, but they come to terms with the fact that life doesn't always work out that way.

This does not, of course, keep them from vigorously pursuing a fair shake, assertively doing all that is necessary to correct an apparent wrong—but they are determined that by all means they will not eat their hearts out if sometimes they cannot be redressed for an obvious wrong. They just do what they can, but they avoid assiduously "the *triple* penalty."

Avoiding triple penalties

The basic penalty, that occasional injustice is sometimes imposed upon us, is not under our own control. But the second and third penalties are totally self-induced.

The second penalty encompasses allowing yourself to become internally upset over the injustice that took place. The third penalty involves hurting yourself still further while trying to "get even."

The following case of John, definitely a noninner-liberated type, illustrates how a person can foolishly take all three penalities instead of just one, a kind of "triple screwing."

John pays his hard-earned cash for an air conditioner from Friendly Franchise, Inc. When the air conditioner is delivered, he finds that certain parts are defective and that it doesn't cool properly. He calls the complaint department of Friendly Franchise. No satisfaction, just promises. He writes to the company president. Still no satisfaction. (By now, poor John realizes that he has been taken.) This represents the basic penalty—unavoidable sometimes, even by the best of us.

While John takes those steps necessary to be redressed for this obvious wrong, he is filled with anger; he is irritated and annoyed. He loses sleep, he yells at his kids, he bemoans his fate. "Damn that Friendly Franchise. What crooks!" All of John's anger and fury (turned inward on himself) represents the second penalty—a screwing that was totally unnecessary for him to inflict upon himself. Inner-liberated persons *never* take the second penalty, because they have learned how to choose the effective thoughts to prevent such *useless* anger and frustration.

Meanwhile, Friendly Franchise holds a special sale on the very same TV set that John has been shopping around for, for months. Friendly Franchise is legitimately selling this set for one hundred dollars less than all the competition. Furthermore, the set is fully guaranteed by the manufacturer. However, John (in spite) thumbs his nose at this opportunity and pays the extra hundred dollars at another store. He has now taken the third penalty—just about all that he can get. He has spited himself in order to get even. An inner-liberated person *never* spites himself in order to get even unless he has weighed the advantages and disadvantages.

In other words, inner-liberated people might get hurt every now and then, but by choosing the necessary effective thoughts they always manage to greatly minimize their loss. This option is open to everyone.

Imagine a world in which so much of the anguish was eliminated overnight, where no one upset himself unnecessarily, and where getting even while spiting oneself rarely took place. What a human ecological event that would be. But there is little hope that *everyone* will operate that way. It is an individual choice. It is an inner-liberated person's policy.

A THOUGHT FOR YOUR FILES (CHOOSE ONE)

Defective Thought

How did my car break down in the middle of nowhere? Bad luck. A rotten deal. I feel miserable and angry.

Effective Thought

Ouch. Look at this strange place where my car broke down. I sometimes set myself up for stupid circumstances. Shit. Oh well, enough of that. How can I turn this into something worthwhile?

Armed now with the basics of how to go about choosing more effective thoughts, you are well prepared to take Centering-Step Two, a step that gives you a greater sense of who you really are. Who is this person choosing these thoughts? Have you ever really defined your real self—on your own terms? What is it that you really want out of your life?

Chapter
· 3 ·
STEP TWO:
Defining Your Inner Self

N ow that you are aware of the tremendous power you
have available to you by choosing your own thoughts
and can readily distinguish between an effective thought
and a defective thought, you are ready to take the second
step toward inner liberation. Soon you will define your
inner self totally on your own terms. But first you must face
and deal with two major issues: what it is that you really
want out of your life; and who are you?

Certainly you know that you are not going to live forever.
The question of what you want out of this life of yours is
urgent. Once you know what it is that you really want, you
will be able to shape your activities in the finite amount of
time accorded you, in a way that helps you realize your
objectives.

A vacation attitude

Your threescore-and-ten or even four- or fivescore years
are not very much when you compare them with the time

that you will be dead (for eternity). So then isn't it reasonable to look upon your lifetime as just a very short vacation away from the billions of years that you will be in so-called eternity?

I have learned to look at my life exactly that way, and such a view has served me in very good stead. And with such an outlook, a "vacation" mentality, I do as much as I can to make the most of it, and conversely, as *little* as I can to spoil it.

Two years ago, in the midst of a very cold New York winter, I went on a week's vacation with my family to Central America. The sun was shining down there, and it was just beautiful being alive. Yet, on the second day out, the bus that was scheduled to take us on a tour was very late. Some of our fellow vacationers carried on as if their lives were coming to an end. They ranted and raved, complaining bitterly to the tour guide, who had little or no power to remedy the unfortunate circumstances. I voiced a firm complaint also, assuming that it might do some good, but I refused to get myself *internally* upset. After all, I was on vacation, and I was just delighted to be away from the cold winter for a few days. Nothing, I had determined in advance, could possibly spoil my vacation. And nothing did. Not the late tour bus, the angry passengers, or anything else. It turned out to be a marvelous trip—because I was determined in advance to make it that way and knew from the start that I would.

I have exactly the same attitude now toward my entire life. Nothing or no one is going to spoil my little vacation from eternity, if I have anything to do with it—and of course the premise of this book is that I have everything to do with it.

Naturally, opportunist that I am, if there is another life offered to me in the hereafter, I'll be glad to accept it, but as for now—well, this life is the "bird in the hand." No waiting for retirement for me before I begin enjoying myself. Right now. Today. This is it. You, too, are on your short vacation and can decide in advance, with determination, that you are going to enjoy it, that you're going to have as satisfying a life as possible.

A THOUGHT FOR YOUR FILES (CHOOSE ONE)

Defective Thought

When I retire, I'd better take up something interesting.

Effective Thought

I'd better take up something really interesting now; something of meaning that can carry me right through so-called retirement.

What Really Satisfies You?

Of course, I am not advocating dropping everything and just going out and raising hell. That may bring you infantile, immediate gratification, but not much of lasting significance. An inner-liberated version of a satisfying personal existence is one where you have a chance to experience qualitatively and in depth the best than any human being is capable of experiencing, in terms of such qualities as "love," excitement," "purpose," and "feeling." The emphasis is firmly biased toward quality rather than quantity. A life of empty hedonism and "more, more" is insufficient for most inner-liberated persons. Although they do not expect to do everything, they do expect a life in which they are able to share with and come close to others, to deal with what life has to offer head on, with vitality and enthusiasm. They do not seek to escape from this, the only life they can be sure of, by sitting it out or watching from the sidelines. They prefer active engagement in life—taking risks, sometimes failing—but always with the will to pick themselves up and become involved again, more intelligently perhaps, but involved nontheless.

A THOUGHT FOR YOUR FILES (CHOOSE ONE)

Defective Thought	**Effective Thought**
I'll seek satisfaction in my inner life later, perhaps. My life will go on.	I definitely will enjoy myself today. Life is very, very short. Shorter, undoubtedly, than most think.

The crucial question about satisfaction is, "What do *you* seek?" What is it that you, personally, desire out of this finite life of yours?

Are you determined to have a high-quality inner life?

Do you hope to have a life filled with nothing but happiness and ecstasy? Too often, those seeking only happiness out of life find that they have taken off in an empty pursuit. Trying hard to be happy makes happiness even more elusive. Happiness serves better as a by-product rather than as an end in itself.

Please take a piece of paper and a pencil, and try the following exercises.

LISTING YOUR WANTS

Assume it is possible for you to have anything at all that you *want* and complete the following list. Throw caution to the winds. Be as greedy as possible (remembering that no one other than you need ever see this list).

I think I want   ———————————————————

  ———————————————————

I think I want   ———————————————————

  ———————————————————

I think I want   _____

_____

I think I want   _____

_____

I think I want   _____

_____

I think I want   _____

_____

I think I want   _____

_____

This list, of course, only represents your thinking now, and it might change if you were to complete such a list at another date. However, your wants as listed indicate something significant about you. They are clues to your life's purposes and goals. They also reflect your values.

Look over your list. Ask yourself the following questions. Is there something missing from the list that I was afraid of putting in? (If so, add it in.) Are these wants reality-based? Which of these are possible and which are wild fantasies? What do my fantasies suggest to me about my deepest aims? What can be done, if anything, to help me achieve these deeper aims? What do my wants reflect about my particular values? Are most of them about people and relationships, my health, travel? Are my wants based on having lots of money or material possessions? What steps must I take to begin to achieve these wants? Have I differentiated between essentials (needs) and nonessentials? (If not, try to make that distinction, since the difference between wants and needs makes a great difference in the amount of pressure you put on yourself to attain them. Generally, basic food, shelter, and clothing are needs, as are "effective thoughts." All else might be preferences or wants worthy of attaining, but not *essential* for existence.)

ONE YEAR, ONE MONTH, ONE DAY TO LIVE

Divide a piece of paper into three equal parts and write on one of the thirds, *One year to live.* Then list the activities you think you would engage in if you were told with authority that you had only one year left to live. Look over your list. What do the actions that you estimated for yourself suggest to you? What are some of the things that are really important to you in this life of yours?

On the next third of the page, write, *One month to live.* Again, project what you would do if you were told by an authority that you had only thirty days left in your life. Analyze this list. In what ways does it differ from the preceding list? Are the items on this list of higher priority than those on your first list?

Finally, head the last third of your paper with the phrase, *Twenty-four hours left to live.* This is it. Very little time left. What do you project you would do if you knew for sure that you had only twenty-four hours left in your life? Would you want to be with a particular person? Would you prefer to be alone? Is there any urgent unfinished business that you would want to take care of? Whom would you call on the phone, if anyone? What would you want to say? What would you do? Would you write, pray, rest, run?

Naturally, it is very difficult to imagine accurately how you would act if you knew that your time was running out in this manner. Still, it is likely that many of your deeply held values and purposes in life have emerged. If you did operate on the premise that you had only a finite amount of time left to you, it is likely that you would undertake the things that are most important to you.

WRITING YOUR OWN EPITAPH

If you were to choose your own epitaph, what would it be? Close your eyes for a moment or two and imagine that you are looking at a gravemarker. It is yours, and something about you is written on it. It reads, HERE LIES (your name). Now fill in the rest on your own. What is it that you would like said about you and your life? You don't have forever to accomplish what you want out of your life, as you well know. If you were not satisfied with your own epitaph at this point, rewrite it immediately—and then spend the rest of your life living up to it.

Inner-liberated goals tend to be down-to-earth and realistic. No miracles are expected or required to attain them. An inner-liberating goal is one that you can achieve without requiring that you manage the thoughts of any other person. It is a cardinal principle that you can take responsibility only for what you yourself choose to think and not for what others choose to think. Therefore, it might be useful for you to evaluate the wants that you listed above, to ascertain whether they can be achieved without relying on anyone else to think a certain way. If any of your wants do require that another person think a certain way, recognize at once that this want is unsuitable in terms of the goal of inner liberation. Rephrase or redevelop your want so that it can be achieved without relying on another person. For example, instead of "wanting a book *published*," revise your goal to "wanting to write an excellent book" (published or not). Or if your want was "to find someone who deeply loves me," revise this goal "to find someone that *I* deeply care about." And so on.

If one of your primary life goals is to live a more satisfying personal existence, you will be pleased to know that you have set a very realistic and attainable goal for yourself!

Once you have fully clarified for yourself just what it is you realistically want out of your life, you can begin to work toward attaining it.

Undoubtedly, a more satisfying personal existence is one of your fundamental wants or you would not be reading this book. Therefore let's see exactly how this *realistic,* down-to-earth (though high-sounding) goal can be readily achieved. In order to do this, it is necessary to become thoroughly familiar with a most important psychological principle—a principle known as the self-fulfilling prophecy.

THE SELF-FULFILLING PROPHECY

The way others see us, and most important, the way that we perceive ourselves, has everything to do with what we shall become. Social scientists have observed that when persons make predictions, they often inadvertently tend to act in such a manner as to make these predictions come true. For example, if I predict that my daughter will behave in a disruptive manner during a car trip, certain nuances of my behavior toward her—perhaps the way that I speak or even look at her—will tend to influence her to behave just as I predicted. Then later I can say to my wife, "See, I told you so."

In California some years ago, a wide-scale experiment was conducted to test the theory of the self-fulfilling prophecy. Teachers were led to expect, through falsified test scores, that students in their classrooms were to have an intellectual growth spurt. Not surprisingly, it was found that most of the students did indeed have such a growth spurt, very much in line with the test prediction. It was only sometime afterward that the teachers learned that the test scores with which they had been furnished were entirely fabricated and randomly supplied.

It is not surprising that so many persons find they can do

much better when they are given a chance to start over again in a totally different environment where the expectations about them are different.

Your prophecy about yourself

The most important prophecy that you can make is the prediction that you make about your inner self. If, for example, you firmly predict that you will be calm in a given stressful situation, the chances are extremely good that, in fact, you will be very calm when the situation arrives. Similarly, you can earnestly predict that you have the inner capacity to artfully dance, write, sing, make love, type, build, manage, or do many of the other things that normal human beings do, and you will find that your prediction about yourself will very likely come true. Of course, you cannot perform miracles: grow another six inches if you are an adult, fly by flapping your arms, or do anything that is out of the realm of possibility.

There are also self-*defeating* prophecies. Negative prophecies, in a similar fashion, tend to come true if you believe them deeply enough. "I won't be able to build, manage, dance, sing, achieve, etc.," can most readily become facts. Therefore, it is important that you make every effort to make *positive*, absolutely realistic predictions about your capabilities and eliminate any negative ones that are self-limiting. Many of us, unfortunately, vastly underestimate our natural, realistic positive capacities. It is sad to think that most persons utilize only a very small percentage of their innate talent to creatively think, work, and play.

Defining Your Inner Self

Philosophers, theologians, and psychologists all agree on one thing: there is absolutely no agreement on the fundamental nature of man. No one really knows whether man is inherently good or evil, or even if man is free or controlled. To my amazement, I found out after years of study and searching that there is no clear agreement on this extremely important issue. For example, Dr. Carl Rogers, a highly respected and influential psychologist, believes that man is inherently good and free. Given a nurturant environment, Rogers says, a man can be expected to grow and flourish. On the other side of the coin is Sigmund Freud, who considers man essentially libidinous and fundamentally primitive. Another noted authority, Dr. B. F. Skinner, holds that man is unfree and only imagines that he has free will. Who is right? None have all the evidence unequivocably on their side. In fact, there are probably as many versions about human nature as there are commentators. The most reasonable explanation I've come across regarding man's nature comes from social scientists who conclude that man is defined more by the social-political system in which he happens to reside than by any other factor.

Are you willing to allow yourself to be defined by a political system? In a totalitarian dictatorship, you are not to be trusted. In a political system such as ours, you are worthy of trust. Fortunately, you live in a democratic society and do not have to rely upon the state to tell you who you are. You can decide, *if* you choose to do so, all on your own.

You are the best authority. Who we are is too important an issue to be left to others. In fact, it can only be answered with absolute authority by *you* and no one else. Of course, there is no shortage of others who will define you if you do not do so yourself. Often these others include well-meaning family members, relatives, friends, and people at work. If you are like most people, you will concede that most of your present identity is not really of your own choosing but rather that it has been unwittingly bestowed upon you by society and others. If your present version of your inner self, your real self, is entirely satisfying, then redefining your inner self entirely on your own terms will probably be of little value. However, if you are not getting all that you think is possible out of your life, then redefining your *inner self* in an inner-liberating fashion will undoubtedly enhance the quality of your personal existence.

Most of us have not taken time out in our lives to clarify what this inner self is really like. Some people's inner selves are very negative and very demanding. "You're no good. You don't deserve better." Others have an inner self that is freeing—liberating. "You're a decent person, you deserve a good life." As important as it is, often the definition has been left to develop in slipshod fashion, and therefore it becomes necessary that you take it upon yourself (rather than leave it to less-qualified others) to define (or redefine) you inner self in such a way that it is your *friend,* your ally, your supporter. This is of prime significance, because it is true that "as you see yourself, you shall become."

If you see yourself as flawed, inept, losing, you can be sure that is what you will be. If you see yourself (at the inner-core level) as possessing inner calm, having excitement and adventure as well as purpose and meaning in your life—then undoubtedly that is the kind of life you will have in store for you.

INNER VS. OUTER SELF

Each of us has two identities, a public or external identity and a private, internal identity. Your external identity is a product of the various "roles" that you play every day: mother or father, worker, executive, Democrat, Republican. Your external identity is important, especially, for managing (or surviving) in the day-to-day world—for raising children, earning a living, and so forth. But your inner identity is even more important. This is the place where you really live. The self that you talk to when you are alone or faced with a problem. And the conversations you have with this your inner self are undoubtedly the most important conversations you can possibly have. If you miss-hit the tennis ball, do you say to yourself, "Damn you. Can't you keep your eye on the ball?" Or do you say, "Well, nice try. Just do better next time." Each of us treats himself differently in similar circumstances.

Who is this self that you speak to, in your mind's eye? It is the *inner* you.

Your inner self is always with you, of course. It is this inner self that you consult and address when you are alone, about to make a decision, when you are worried, creating, or doing. Sometimes this inner self of yours acts as an ally, a friend. And sometimes not. Sometimes we treat it roughly. ("Damn you. Why did you do that? You know better.") And less often, we treat it kindly. ("You know, you're really a nice guy. I'm proud of you.")

You, of course, are only one person—a person depending on the quality and character of our inner selves, we can be one of three types: inner-liberated; outer-dominated; or outer-controlled.

Inner-liberated persons have a very strong, healthy, free, inner self as I have shown in the diagram that follows. The white space is the outer self, and the darkened area represents the inner self. Notice that generous portions of the healthy inner self spill over to the surface.

Being *dominated* by the externals of life (job, money, image, material possessions, etc.) is not as negative as being *controlled* by them. The outer-dominated person is as follows:

Notice that the wall on the outside is much thicker. The core of inner self is smaller and almost totally confined, but with some outlets. The outer-dominated person, I suppose, includes the vast majority of people. He has a flawed vision of his inner self. He feels a bit trapped, a bit confused, and he says, "But that's the way it is." And we, of course, the inner-liberated persons above, would disagree with him.

The outer-*controlled* person is really a victim of anything external he happens to encounter. He is totally defined by externals, having little or no recognition of the fact that the potential for a strong inner self even exists. He has no capacity for introspecting. His name, his job title, his social roles are everything. Seen graphically, he looks like this:

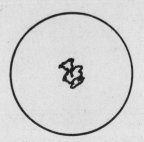

Much of your present identity has been derived from "roles" and years of conditioning. Your present general identity has been derived largely from your contacts with presumably well-meaning parents, teachers, and friends. Even your children, if you have any, have probably taken a crack at defining you as well. "Daddy," his daughter said with annoyance, "do you want to know what I think of you as a father?" "Sure, darling, please tell me who I am," he might respond, as he listened with guilt. Most of your present identity, however, was probably determined before the age of five. It is in those early years that we are most impressionable. Your definition of your inner self, if it has been defined at all, was more than likely not really of your own choosing. Even something as personal as your given name is not of your own choosing. My ears literally perk up when I hear my name—just like Pavlov's dog. Nothing more than a conditioned response! All of us are products of heavy conditioning. Even much of the clothing that we ostensibly choose to wear, our little mannerisms, and perhaps even the way that we walk and talk, are the result of long-time conditioning. There are all kinds of models and reinforcers bearing down on us. We've been managed and processed, (call it socialization) ever since birth, facing innumerable authority figures, massive advertising and sloganeering, and all kinds of influential suggestions that badger us day after day on TV and in print. It is no wonder that the question "Who are you?" tends to intimidate when we ask this of our inner selves.

Last year, Margarie, a thirty-five-year-old housewife with three children and an uncaring husband, came to me for counseling, in a very confused state of mind. "About four years ago, I had a complete nervous breakdown," she said, "and I turned myself in at the local mental hospital. I was there for a period of two weeks, and eventually, with the help of chemotherapy, my depression lifted somewhat—and I was released of my own accord. But since then, I've been barely managing to get by, day by day, and since my breakdown, I've *discarded all the roles* I had been given—but I still don't know who I am. Sure, I was given a very rigid upbringing, and I was very religious. I wasn't even permitted to think 'improper' thoughts. Well, after my breakdown, I discarded all that. I no longer wanted to be the perfect mother, the perfect wife—the perfect anything.

"But now that I've discarded all that—I'm still left with the question 'Who am I?' I frankly don't know." Margarie did not find the identity she had been given sufficiently serviceable. She had no backup identity that went beyond these social roles.

WHO ARE YOU?

In a sense, the question "Who are you?" is almost unfair to ask. Yet it is precisely this question that you must answer with clarity if you ever hope to define your inner self on your own terms. Have you ever really tried to define your inner self on your own terms. Have you ever really tried to define yourself your way? Your inner self is certainly not your job title, so you cannot comfortably hide behind that. Job titles are external, not inner, descriptions of self. Nor is your inner self the other social roles that you might have. Your inner self is much deeper than these conventional social roles.

You may be saying, "Wait, I know who I am. I'm me." But just who is that vague, extremely ambiguous, quite amorphous "me" to whom you refer? It is essential that you at long last define your inner self in a unique, original, and satisfying manner. Only then can you set in motion a productive prophecy for yourself that will lead to your own inner liberation.

During a recent centering seminar that I conducted, each member of the group suggested identities for the inner selves of the others. But, finally it was left for each member to choose his own inner identity. Song and book titles, countries, even names of famous paintings, have been effectively used to describe this part of self. The names selected are only a symbol of one's private version of self. Certainly job titles, social roles, even our given names, tend to place us into "little boxes," boxes that sometimes seriously limit our potential. So in order to escape from such boxes you must take on a new version of you.

The client Margarie, cited earlier, who lost track of who she was after she dropped her conventional roles, created a very exciting secret inner identity for herself during the course of my counseling with her. This new inner identity of hers, that she herself created, proved infinitely more serviceable that the social roles that others had foisted on her—and which resulted in her nervous breakdown.

Margarie described her secret new identity as follows: "I see a beautiful white bird, a dove, flying with an olive branch in one of its claws. I can remember early in my life admiring such a bird. This dove is circling gracefully round and round above a sturdy boat, a boat that is moving purposefully along in a calm, blue sea. The boat seems to be heading somewhere, somewhere significant, somewhere worthwhile. Somehow I sense this boat will be able to make it safely through all kinds of weather, waters calm and waters rough. I find this a very soothing picture. And this *whole* picture is me."

For Margarie, this secret inner identity acted as the center point around which she was able to balance the many confusing facets of her real-life situation as mother, wife, P.T.A. officer, and person. When things become complex or upsetting for her, as they sometimes do, she shuts her eyes and returns to her inner vision of herself—for solace, for support, for direction.

I, too, have a picture of my inner self that has served me countless times in very good stead.

Quite recently, for example, I was required to wait in a long line at the New York Motor Vehicle Bureau in order to register a car. The line seemed endless, and my own paranoia made me believe that the clerks were deliberately spiting me because I was in a hurry. Then, suddenly, I realized that I was getting my insides in a tumult. "What kind of way is this for a Gentle-Flowing Brook (my definition of my inner self) to operate?" I thought, "I'm acting more like a damned roaring ocean." Then I got in touch with what I was thinking and feeling—and made it a point to take charge.

I closed my eyes for a moment and clearly visualized in my mind's eye a beautiful, crystal-clear, gently flowing brook, a brook that I remember experiencing one summer in the Smoky Mountains. My whole body slowed down. Gentle, flowing. Ease. Calm. Moving gently—someplace— who knows where; to a larger body of clear water perhaps. And as you can imagine, my whole system slowed down. Gone was the roaring ocean. And there I stood ever so calmly and comfortably in line—waiting my turn. Enjoying sight, sound, feeling, being alive. And all at no charge. Definitely a personal ecological event. Treating yourself decently is no reason to feel guilty; it is a social contribution. And all at no charge—a quiet, qualitative, inner-liberating experience. You don't have to try to improve the whole world to improve the lot of mankind.

Once equipped with a very clear image of your inner self, never again will you be caught fumbling when asking yourself "Who am I really?" You will be able to answer in terms of your inner-self definition, not in terms of those social-role games that most persons are limited to. Remember, if you don't define yourself this way, there are plenty of other persons, well-meaning and not so well-meaning, who will be more than glad to do so, as they have been doing for years.

In my own mind, with my own private name for my inner self—Gentle-Flowing Brook—I imagine a very special, particularly beautiful brook, flowing along, lightly, easily, sometimes through rough areas, yet always moving along. The brook is flowing somewhere that is very worthwhile, eventually uniting with a large body of water, a crystal-clear, blue glacier lake. This image that I have found offers me hope, providing as it does for my uniting with something larger than myself. The gentle flowing of the brook symbolizes for me the inner calm that I so cherish. Also, its spontaneous turns through forests and its small waterfalls for me symbolize adventure. When needed, I can draw great nourishment from this special vision of inner self that I alone created. I find this self-picture comforting, reassuring, and revitalizing, and I take pride in the fact that this version of myself is one that is totally of my own design and choosing. No one else in the entire world can define myself better than I can. And I have.

YOUR INNER METAPHOR

In order to create a clear inner-self picture, permit your imagination free reign. Use metaphors if you like, metaphors from nature, art, literature, everyday life. Even images of cars or TV products are fair game. You are restricted only by the limits of your imagination. It is important, before you tackle this self-imaging task, that you fully appreciate its significance. Remember, for example, that the picture you see need not symbolize you as you *are* but rather as you would like to become. Later you will see why elements of inner calm, purpose, and adventure are important parts of this image, but try to include them now —even if the reason is not yet absolutely clear to you.

The picture that you are about to imagine should have some elements of quiet and peace connected with it—signifying the inner calm that the inner-liberated person finds so necessary. In addition, try to have your picture reflect a sense of hope, of going somewhere—a sense of purpose. Also include movement in your vision—to symbolize adventure, the third element of inner liberation.

Find a comfortable position; then shut your eyes and permit your imagination free play for five minutes and see what you can come up with. Don't worry about doing it "right" because if you don't like what you see just now, you can try any time you like later on—and then use the best of your various imaginative creations.

Once you are able to create successfully a vital picture of your inner self, you have established the basis for your own self-fulfilling prophecy. Whenever you find that you are confused or anxious or in a "box" not of your own choosing, you can turn to this self-picture for support, clarification, and nourishment. Without such a picture, you are easy prey for capricious whims of society and very limiting social definitions upon which you are temped to predicate your life. Isn't it far better to have a concept of your inner self that is completely of your own creation rather than having to rely on what others, caring or not, have foisted upon you? As you return to this inner picture of self, time and again, it becomes the real "you." But wait. How about a name for this new version of you, a handle, so that you can remind yourself more conveniently who you really are whenever you need to do so?

Choose your own "handle"

Below are some adjectives and nouns that can be used in various combinations to give your inner-liberated inner self an appropriate name. The list is only suggestive. You might have your own ideas for such a name.

Some Inner-Liberating Adjectives		Some Inner-Liberating Nouns	
Gentle	High	Stream	Rolls Royce
Easy	Free	Eagle	Leaf
Rolling	Clear	Seagull	Opera
Mellow	True	Bike	Castle
Flowing	Flexible	Rose	Heart
Centering	Calm	Seeker	Spirit
Feeling	Balanced	Dancer	Brook
Healthy	Adventurous	Flowerbed	Ocean

Lively	Rambling	Song	Mountain
New	Open	Boat	Flower
Loving	Caring	Cloud	Apple
Warm	Calming	Forest	Dawn

Try out various combinations to see how they sound. A new name by itself serves little purpose; it needs an image that goes along with it. Perhaps the name you select can supplement the image you already focused upon, or better still, help this inner-self picture of yours still more. Make up a few names and try them on for size. Again, you're not limited to this list but come up, at least tentatively, with a "handle" for your inner self. Take a few minutes and *do this now*. Have some fun in the process. Experiment. If you don't find what you've done completely satisfying, try again. I cannot emphasize enough how important it is that you have a very clear and imaginative picture of your inner self, how useful a *name* for this picture is in helping you remind yourself who you really are when circumstances warrant such a reminder. It is so easy to be pulled off center by your job, by many of life's circumstances, even by your family. But if you know who you are at the inner-self level, you will become immune to the traps, boxes, and conditions that often confuse most others. "After all," you will think to yourself, "why does a Lively Forest have to become upset over that?"

Another one of my clients, Lester, a fifty-eight-year-old tax accountant who had suffered a heart attack a year before coming to me for counseling applied this method. Lester defined his inner self as Flowerbed. He said that he chose flowerbed because he always loved gardening, although he had little time to work at this love of his. "As a flowerbed, I see things grow, and then when they die, they soften the bed, add to it, make it more fertile and possible for new plants to spring forth. I find, being a flowerbed, that I am now more resilient and hopeful than I ever was before. Unfortunately, my heart attack was brought on because I took the pressures of my tax work too seriously. Also I always felt that my family puts lots of pressure on me as a father, as a husband. It was too much. Now during tax time, when some of my crazy clients get all upset, I think to myself, 'What's getting upset over taxes and deadlines got to do with being a flowerbed?' I'm more relaxed now than I've ever been in my entire life. I only wish I knew that I was a flowerbed before I got my attack." Chances are, if he had, such an attack might have been avoided.

Even if you haven't made a final decision as to your new name, make a tentative one. Write it down in the margin of this book. Then check it out later and see if you still like it. If it doesn't quite suit you then, change it. Find one that does. It can mean a life.

YOUR SELF-PICTURE

It is important that you never forget who you are. So that you can reinforce this, ask yourself the two following questions periodically: *"What is it that I want out of my life?"* (Remember to separate your desires from your needs); (2nd) *"Who am I?"* (Shut your eyes, return to that inner picture of you, and experience it with your whole being). Then mention your secret name to yourself to remind yourself who you really are, regardless of what others might call you.

Having defined yourself on your own terms, knowing more about what it is that you want out of your life, and having learned how to consciously choose your own thoughts, you are now centered in an extremely powerful position. But with this power comes a new responsibility.

You must determine whether you really want to center yourself toward an inner-liberated lifestyle—since other interesting lifestyle options are also open to you now. Before you decide for sure that the inner-liberated way of life is really for you, let's take a closer look at the new options you now have.

Chapter
· 4 ·
STEP THREE:
Committing Yourself to Inner Liberation

D ecision time. Is inner liberation really for you? Having learned how to choose your own effective thoughts and having defined your inner self in a new way, several interesting options open up to you. Therefore, before you decide that you really want to go on toward inner liberation, it is wise to pause, to consider these other options. Then, if you still decide to opt for inner liberation, you'll have some sense at least of what options you are leaving behind.

Knowing what you now do, you can opt for a life that is totally hedonistic—a playboy kind of existence. It is possible to regularly choose thoughts that would keep you that way. My concern about that way of life is that it too often ends up empty, a trip to nowhere. A second option is the life of the ascetic, observing life from a distance and choosing thoughts that support your observations. This might be satisfying enough for some, but it's certainly not for me. I prefer mixing it up in the real world, living life firsthand as much as possible rather than as an outside observer.

No lifestyle I can think of offers deeper satisfactions than the inner-liberated lifestyle. The satisfaction from inner liberation far exceeds the satisfaction you could expect from either the playboy or the ascetic lifestyle. There are three distinct parts of an inner-liberated person's life that offer generous amounts of deep, inner satisfaction: he has a full measure of inner calm in his life; he lives a life that is characterized by purpose and meaning; there is plenty of excitement and adventure in his life. That's it in a nutshell. Calm, purpose, and adventure. Doesn't that kind of life appeal to you?

Balancing Effective Thoughts

A thought which proves satisfying to an inner-liberated person must assist this person in achieving any one of the three dimensions in his life—calm, purpose, or adventure—without in the slightest impairing his sustaining any of the others. If a given thought helps me attain an improved measure of inner calm, it must not at the same time interfere with my capacity for adventure or sense of personal purpose or it will not prove satisfying to me. If a given thought gives me a sense of greater adventure—such as "I'm not showing up for work today, but instead I'm heading for the beach"—it must not interfere with my sense of inner calm or larger life purposes, for then it cannot be effective. An effective thought requires a judicious balancing of all three of the prime dimensions of inner liberation.

CALM

The deepening of your level of inner calm (explained in detail in the next chapter) is the next stage in the six-step centering process that leads to your personal inner liberation. Inner peace, an abiding harmony between oneself and the rest of the world, even the universe, is clearly a noble and readily attainable goal as you shall see. Commonly, prayer and pills are the most popular routes to calming oneself. But the route taken by inner liberationists is drug-free, and although meditation and prayer are by no means ruled out, they are not the primary means employed. Rather, in keeping with the principle of thought choice, you will learn to choose the appropriate *effective thoughts* that lead you to whatever level of calm you desire. It's easier done than said.

PURPOSE

Having attained an agreeable level of inner calm, Centering-Step Five is to clarify your personal purposes and priorities. A life without clear purposes too often adds up to life void of meaning. There is no reason to live a life that goes in circles, that is aimless and vague.

ADVENTURE

And finally, Centering-Step Six on the path to inner liberation is the most joyful, the most exciting of all. Here you learn to heighten the level of excitement and adventure in your life. After all, a life without adventure yields no joy, no humor, no emotion, no feeling, ecstasy, exhilaration, surprise—the essential ingredients in any life worthy of being called life. Such a life requires adventure and risk.

The inner-liberated person is like a ship that is steaming its way to a distant port. The ship is inner-liberated if it is a sturdy ship aboard which there is calm, if it is actively engaging the high seas, and if it has a clear mission to deliver its cargo safely to the port of destination. Without calm or the active movement through the seas or the sense of mission, the ship becomes less than effective. Clearly, a ship with all three of these dimensions is functioning optimally—as is a person with all three of these dimensions.

Undoubtedly, there are times when people experience inner calm, times when they sense adventure and excitment, and other times when they know exactly what their mission is. But when a person experiences all of these dimensions at once and regularly, he is well on his way to inner liberation.

Putting a full measure of these three dimensions into your life often requires some personality change. Interestingly, it is readily possible that by exercising your power of thought choice you can create for yourself a fully inner-liberated personality. Here's how you will be enabled to do that.

CREATE YOUR OWN PERSONALITY TRAITS

If you choose certain thoughts consistently and act upon these thoughts with regularity, you will develop a pattern. Such patterns become personality traits. If you regularly think of yourself as "effectively lovable" and act that way consistently, lovable you will become. It's a self-fulfilling prophecy. The traits that lead to inner liberation can be yours by regularly choosing the necessary thoughts. It is possible to achieve all kinds of personality traits this way, some helpful and others not. In fact, you have developed your traits this way all of your life. What is new here is that you are now going to be more selective in the type of traits that you acquire for yourself.

All inner-liberating personality traits can be achieved without having to rely on anyone else's thinking, feeling, or behaving in a particular way. Some of the traits that do not meet this test include such attractive qualities as "admirable," "charming," "respected," and "liked." They can never be attained independently, and therefore they are not appropriate goals in themselves. It is possible that you might achieve them anyhow, but only as a fringe benefit. The fact is that these kinds of qualities most often come easier to you if you do not try too hard to get them. They are much like the butterfly that you chase—when you give up, it often settles gently on your shoulder of its own accord.

Inner-liberating personality traits are achieved without the necessity of anything supernatural or unnatural. You don't need to be especially lucky, or to be discovered, you don't have to win the lottery or inherit money. Nor are any major miracles needed. You will not have to grow a few inches if you are an adult, make someone rise up from the grave, acquire a great talent and then become famous, or defy the laws of gravity—and if you decide to walk on water, it will only be because you are very much aware of where the rocks are.

Each of the personality traits that you will add to your profile will clearly assist you in becoming inner-liberated. The new trait must be geared to one or more of the three dimensions of calm, purpose, or adventure. "Happy," "perfect," and "striving" are traits that are not in themselves inner-liberating qualities. As you will see, some qualities which seem most attractive on the surface are not really all that they appear.

The inner-liberating personality traits are subject to misunderstanding; if they are misunderstood, they can be abused. Therefore, in order that you might avoid any misunderstanding, I have usually prefaced each of them with the adjective "effective" and then explained their special meaning in detail. For example, there are times when it can be disastrous to be perfectly honest (one of the attributes), such as when a supersensitive person asks you your opinion of his performance and you may not wish to hurt this person unnecessarily or cramp this person's style of learning. Thus, being honest is not as simple a policy as it might seem.

APPLYING EFFECTIVE THINKING

Here is a story that demonstrates inner-liberated thought processes in action.

Don got up early one morning to discover that his house had been burglarized overnight. Many of his most treasured possessions had been taken. Don was quite shaken. But only for a very short time. He reminded himself that he was on his vacation from eternity, and he had long before come to appreciate the fact that he could not ever really be certain that he could keep all of his material possessions for his entire life. He had often thought to himself, "Every material thing I have is in actuality rented. I *own* only my body and mind." He had also *worked-through* in his mind that there's really very little in the way of absolute justice that he could ever expect to count on (a process that I call "mourning in advance"). Therefore, in keeping with his inner-liberated vow to have as satisfying an inner life as is humanly possible, he deftly proceeded to choose the most effective thoughts to keep himself from driving his fist through the wall out of rage. He quickly and directly acknowledged his *shock* and his (then) strong angry feelings, cursed deeply, but ever so briefly. The effective thoughts almost immediately removed the *cause* of the upset (his mindset), and he began reminding himself consistently to continue to choose thoughts that were going to do him some good. It is true that for a moment or two, every now and then, he would forget and choose a counterproductive thought or two (after all, he is only human and far from perfect)—but for the most part, he handled it all *very* effectively. Calmly, he called the police, gave them whatever information he could (inner-liberated persons are quite assertive), and then he began systematically to straighten out the mess created by the incident.

Don, you will notice, did not *deny* any of the feelings of anger and outrage that he first experienced. (After all, prepared as he was for some injustice in life, he was still caught off guard). He simply expressed these normal emotional reactions (in view of his mindset) quickly and then, with effective thoughts, eliminated much if not all of the basis for anger (having mourned and lamented long before this incident about most of the *sad,* but realistic, facts of life). As quickly as possible, Don made it his vital business to have as satisfying a day as possible—in spite of the "unjust" start.

It is possible that even with all my parenthetical remarks this illustration appears too facile. Yet let me point out at once that there are many people in this world, some of whom you probably know quite well, who have learned quickly to transcend certain influences that would drive another person up the proverbial wall. It is important to remember that Don was not short in his supply of assertiveness, having called the police and done all he could to attain justice; but he did not let the mechanical and necessary steps in assertiveness dampen in any way the satisfaction that was and is his primary goal each day.

I will leave it to you at this point to decide whether or not the inner liberation lifestyle sounds sufficiently attractive for you to pursue it further. But before you make this decision, let me caution you about some of the problems you should anticipate, should you (when you) attain this excellent way of life.

As you must realize, various persons have a vested interest in seeing that you remain exactly the way that you are. If you choose to modify your self-concept, to enjoy a new sense of inner freedom, and consequently, to modify somewhat the way that you customarily behave, I would like to urge you to proceed gently with those around you. It is likely that some will become a bit threatened by your change to greater self-reliance. Try to share your new insights firmly, yet gently and empathically. There is no reason to be reckless with or haughty toward the feelings of others. One of the most significant aspects of an inner-liberated life is that you are a loving person, listening to and caring for others *on their terms.* This does not mean that you will have to compromise any aspect of your inner satisfaction. It merely requires that you remind yourself that all persons are, in a genuine sense, part of you and part of a world that you may not have chosen, but the only one in which you live.

There are those who, in spite of all your efforts to listen and care, will still call you selfish. The label "selfish" is often used to press you into feeling guilty and to have you return to exactly the same positions that you previously held. If someone is worried about your new outlook, remind them that your position is firmly based on listening to and caring for others, but that it in no way includes your expecting to tell them what thoughts to choose.

The Inner Liberation Self-Test

Everyone possesses qualities of inner liberation, but in varying degrees. The following self-administered quiz can give you some idea as to the extent to which you are presently inner-liberated. Of course it is essential that you be as honest with yourself as possible if the score is to be valid. If you take this quiz again about three weeks after you've finished this book, you can expect to see progress—real progress.

Rate yourself by circling the number that most closely approximates your feelings in terms of agreement or disagreement with each statement.

(1) I am seldom preoccupied with thoughts and imaginings regarding the bad things that might happen to me and others, either tomorrow, next week, or years later.

Agree				Uncertain				Disagree
9	8	7	6	5	4	3	2	1

(2) I make it my business to have a great deal of personal satisfaction in my life.

Agree				Uncertain				Disagree
9	8	7	6	5	4	3	2	1

(3) I firmly believe that I, and no one or nothing else, am responsible for the way I feel.

Agree				Uncertain				Disagree
9	8	7	6	5	4	3	2	1

(4) I prefer facing the facts, even when they might be very hard facts, rather than be deluded or delude myself.

Agree				Uncertain				Disagree
9	8	7	6	5	4	3	2	1

(5) I listen deeply to and care for certain other persons on their own terms without imposing my values on them or judging them. I am a loving person.

Agree				Uncertain				Disagree
9	8	7	6	5	4	3	2	1

(6) I tend not to carry grudges, and I get over my own anger rapidly.

Agree				Uncertain				Disagree
9	8	7	6	5	4	3	2	1

(7) I currently have what is to me "a very important project" under way. This project gives me much meaning and is not subjected to any significant outside interferences.

Agree				Uncertain				Disagree
9	8	7	6	5	4	3	2	1

(8) I am involved in a program, either formally or informally, of adequate physical care.

Agree				Uncertain				Disagree
9	8	7	6	5	4	3	2	1

(9) I really enjoy the time that I have on my own. I value being with myself.

Agree				Uncertain				Disagree
9	8	7	6	5	4	3	2	1

(10) I take exciting risks regularly. I very recently took one, and I can be expected to voluntarily take another sometime today or in the near future.

Agree				Uncertain				Disagree
9	8	7	6	5	4	3	2	1

(11) I know very clearly who my inner self is—and I like my inner self.

Agree				Uncertain				Disagree
9	8	7	6	5	4	3	2	1

(12) I tend to search for deeper meaning in life, rather than to pursue happiness.

Agree				Uncertain				Disagree
9	8	7	6	5	4	3	2	1

(13) I am not overly concerned about whether others approve of me or my projects.

Agree				Uncertain				Disagree
9	8	7	6	5	4	3	2	1

(14) I have a great zest for living my life to the fullest, and I do!

Agree				Uncertain				Disagree
9	8	7	6	5	4	3	2	1

(15) I know how to, and do control my own thoughts, feelings, and actions in such a way that gives me a great deal of personal satisfaction.

Agree				Uncertain				Disagree
9	8	7	6	5	4	3	2	1

SCORING: Total all the numbers that you circled.

125–135   Very high. You are in a good position. You can expect this book to be very supportive to your present outlook.

120–124   Very good score. You appear to be well on your way to inner-liberated living. Check over the questions and locate the ones in which you indicate the least agreement. These represent areas that might need some additional attention.

60–119   You scored in the middle range, and therefore it seems likely that you can move either toward or away from inner liberation. The direction, of course, depends on you.

59 or less   You scored low on this test. One positive aspect of this is that you apparently have not tried to deceive yourself about the degree of inner liberation that you currently manifest. You can really apply the principles found in this book toward a more satisfying lifestyle. Please continue to learn.

Chapter
· 5 ·
STEP FOUR:
Attaining Calm

Many are searching for inner calm, harmony, and peace of mind. Seekers of tranquility have resorted to all kinds of approaches in their search, some reasonable (meditation, yoga, a few months on an ashram) and some less than reasonable (self-abusive use of alcohol, drugs, and other means of sheer escapism).

However, the calm of the inner-liberated person is generally achieved without resorting to any of these. He chooses the necessary thoughts to make himself calm, and he has two personality traits in particular which have freed him from much of the inner tension that plagues most people. He learns by choosing the appropriate thoughts, how to be realistically lovable and effectively open.

What do these three people all have in common?

Daryl was a veritable Don Juan, a master of the singles scene, the slick seducer. Women weren't people to Daryl. They were just bodies, flesh, opportunities for conquest.

Clara worried frantically everytime her husband went out

of town on a business trip. Was he really loyal? She also worried every time he so much as talked to another attractive woman.

Alan was very funny. Too funny after a while. He made jokes about everything. Always on. A regular Don Rickles. After a while, you would want to get as far away from him as possible.

Answer: all of them in their own special way would benefit tremendously by choosing more effective thoughts about their own "lovability." ·

Lovability

Each and every one of us was born lovable. We were small, cuddly, dependent, held, nurtured, succored, caressed. We were appreciated, cared for, and listened to, simply because we existed. Feeling and being lovable was part of our basic endowment, a natural birthright. But then, it seems, for many of us this natural quality slipped into limbo, and much of that very positive feeling about how adorable we were (as newborns) seemed to dissipate. Here is how that dissipation process probably works:

The infant at birth might think to itself, "It's just wonderful being as lovable as I am. I appreciate being cared for and attended to." Then, usually quite inadvertently, there will be some occasions when his genuine needs go unmet. A pinched diaper or a pang of hunger—and this time with no mother in immediate attendance. So then it is only natural that the infant innocently begins to choose some untrue thoughts, thoughts that later prove to be counterproductive. He thinks, "Am I not quite as acceptable as I first thought I was?" Of course, it is practically impossible to tend to every single need that an infant and small child have. Yet the small child doesn't realize that, and some very unfortunate ideas continue to form in his mind. He loses some (sometimes much) of the confidence that he once had in the immutable fact that he is lovable. Relatively few persons arrive at adulthood with their initially high feelings of self-esteem fully intact.

But whether your sense of lovability is high or low, all defective thoughts you have about it can be easily neutralized simply by rethinking, this time more accurately, the truth about this most important human quality. You need to store up a generous supply of effective self-esteem thoughts so that you can choose them whenever you need them.

All the word "lovable" means is "the ability to be loved." To be able to be loved requires no special talent other than that you learn to appreciate and respect yourself, "warts and all." It takes no special good looks, no special effort. This is a natural right vested at birth—an out and out gift —and it is probably the most important personal attribute that you can possess. Yet so many have forgotten that they were given a full measure of this quality at birth.

Since love is central to the concept of lovability, let us take a moment to define it. According to inner-liberation standards, love simply means deep listening to and caring for another person on that person's own terms. It is not something that you fall into or that you go out and get. Listening to and caring for another without judging or being critical has always been a rare commodity and seems to be especially rare these days when so many are almost totally preoccupied with themselves.

If you want greater self-esteem, it is important that you make yourself available to be listened to and cared for on your own terms (i.e., loved). Some people are so afraid that no one will ever really appreciate them for what they are that they rarely, if ever, let their guard down and share their feelings. And if a person tends to act in this "unlovable" way, then unlovable he tends to become—another instance of the self-fulfilling prophecy. If a person is overly self-protective, he sends out many signals that keep potential lovers away. The message is, "I'm out-of-bounds."

Joanne, an attractive woman in her mid-twenties, was distraught because her fiancé, for no apparent reason and with no advance warning whatsoever, suddenly left her cold. She came to me in shock. "He wouldn't even tell me why," she said numbly. For a long while after this incident, Joanne was extremely guarded and overly cautious about men. It was practically impossible for her to chance another relationship—although she received a number of warm advances. Joanne could just not bring herself to trust very easily, and it became clear that she felt unworthy of love.

The fact that Joanne felt so unlovable eventually manifested itself in a number of subtle ways. The corners of her mouth were tight. Her body carriage signaled to others, "Stay away!" Even her walk began to betray how poorly she felt about herself. Men she dated seemed to sense her lack of self-esteem. She was saying in essence, "Stay away from me. I don't feel that I am able to be cared for, to be appreciated." Yet, of course, Joanne desperately longed to be appreciated and cared for, to be loved.

Eventually, with the help of counseling, Joanne regained much of her sense of self-esteem. She launched a four-stage assault on her attitude. In the first stage she learned how to choose effective "lovability" thoughts. She came to appreciate her natural attractiveness despite the fact that her so-called lover had deserted her. "How can I be responsible for what he did?" she was able to say.

Joanne was shown how to turn her problem into a project. She began to remind herself regularly that she was just as lovable as any other human being, that she was born that way, and that she still was that way if only she would fully appreciate that she was. Whenever she forgot and let a negative thought intrude, she would counter it and eventually replace it with thoughts that led to greater self-esteem. For example, "I feel warm and attractive" would be used to counter and replace "I feel cold and distant." Of course, this in itself was not enough in Joanne's case. Her feeling of rejection was so deeply felt that she needed to work-through some of the anger and disappointment she had experienced when her so-called lover abandoned her.

This brings us, then, to the second stage in Joanne's project. She had to learn how to "cool" an overactive counterproductive thought: "I'm unlovable because I've been abandoned."

WORKING-THROUGH

Each of us learns at his own rate. I believe that most of us can learn almost anything—given sufficient time. And when it comes to intelligent social behavior, some of us learn much more quickly than others. Joanne was a fast learner. She had to learn that although it was now too late to tell her former lover how angry and disgusted she was with his behavior, she could still express this anger with dispatch and finish with much of it. It was important that Joanne be given the opportunity to work-through this unexpressed and unresolved anger, rather than continue to use it counterproductively. Unexpressed and unresolved anger often is turned on oneself and can lead to deep depression. Or else the unresolved anger is projected onto undeserving others—in Joanne's case, some of the men that she tried dating.

The fact that she was able to acknowledge her anger toward her ex-lover was very important. Many hurt persons experience denial when in the midst of a loss. Dr. Kübler-Ross, in her landmark book *Death and Dying,* enumerated five developmental steps that the dying person needs help in working-through regarding his own death. I have found these very same five steps are extremely useful in helping people work-through losses of all kinds, be they losses on the job, in the family, or of lovers, as in the case of Joanne.

These five steps are worth reviewing here, for they apply to any serious personal problems of loss that you might want to work-through on your own. The steps are: (1) denial; (2) bargaining; (3) anger; (4) depression; and (5) acceptance. They do not always occur in this sequence. In Joanne's case, she first used denial. She thought, when first abandoned by her lover, "This isn't really happening to me. He'll be back." She was unrealistic, denying what really happened for over three months before it actually dawned upon her what had actually taken place. She then bargained, as she vowed, "Please, God, give me another chance. Bring him back. I'll be so much nicer to him. Please, I'll change." Of course as bargaining proved unworkable, she became angry. Then when she realized what had happened, she became hurt and angry, then depressed.

After a period of being low, Joanne was enabled to move toward eventual acceptance of her loss, thus completing the five steps of working-through. However, in Joanne's case, there was still a good deal of unfinished business that required resolution before she was able to move comfortably to complete acceptance of her loss.

The ways of resolving this unfinished business are various. One of the techniques that I employed with Joanne was to have her, at a propitious moment, pretend that she was telling her former lover exactly how angry she was with him. Sometimes, as it was with Joanne, strong emotional expression is almost a complete catharsis, and much, if not all, of the anger dissipates. Many things can then be appreciated with a new perspective, a new mindset. Once this begins to happen, counterproductive thoughts cool down and it becomes much easier to overwhelm such unpleasant thoughts with more effective thoughts.

However, there are bound to be occasions in life when you are caught unprepared, that is, not having worked through in advance an effective line of thought so that you can function optimally. Whenever you find yourself too angry, or depressed, or nervous, you must pull yourself aside (mentally) and work through an effective line of thinking for yourself.

This working-through process can be accomplished in most cases without the help of a therapist. In fact, by rethinking many of the issues about life, we can prevent ourselves from ever having to experience the kind of anger that for a time overwhelmed Joanne. And if anger is not repressed, because it never existed, then it requires no working-through.

As part of the working-through process, Joanne learned to appreciate certain facts of life. Armed with these new facts, she was able to prevent herself from ever again going through the deep emotional pain that she had experienced from this rejection. For example, Joanne came to accept fully the fact that in life, although we can sometimes get very close to another, there is still part of us that will always be very much alone. This was not easy for her to accept, because ever since she was a small child she had expected a much more romantic vision of life, with Prince Charming sweeping her off her feet, the two of them becoming one. It was difficult for her to give up this dream. But when she did, she became free, and once again was able to risk closeness—to leave herself open to being appreciated and cared for. At the same time she recognized that she was an autonomous individual, lovable whether someone else loved her or not. Her attitude came to be, "Whether I have a close and intimate relationship in my life or not, I am still going to have a very satisfying personal existence." And, as so often happens when a person stops trying too hard, a number of warm and loving relationships began to come her way.

While all this was going on, Joanne was also actively engaged in another important part of her redevelopment.

This called for her to be actively engaged in a challenging activity that did not require the approval of anyone but herself. The project that Joanne undertook was gardening. She began to study avidly about all kinds of flower bulbs and how to plant them. She went on several garden tours to learn more. She was consumed by her project, and so she was able to transcend some of the unhappiness she was experiencing and began to reestablish important feelings of self-worth and pride.

The last step, going out into the world of intimate relationships with men, was no longer such a great threat. There are, in my files, case after case of persons that I came to know very well, who have, through a process very similar to the one that I have just described, been enabled to turn around the direction of their lives.

Just because you are lovable there is still no guarantee that any other human being will fully appreciate and take advantage of this fact. But it is absolutely impossible for you to be responsible for what another chooses to think and feel. It's a full-time job keeping your own thought file in order, let alone managing someone else's.

A THOUGHT FOR YOUR FILES (CHOOSE ONE)

Defective Thought	Effective Thought
Oh, what a nice gift so and so gave me. What can I give her appropriately in return?	Oh, what a nice gift so and so gave me. Thank you very much.

REJECTING REJECTION

Inner-liberated persons have a very useful way of looking at situations that others might interpret as rejection. Their attitude is reflected in the following soliloquy:

"It's very difficult for me to be rejected by anyone. If someone says she doesn't like me or something I've done, I hardly ever take it personally. After all, it's not me that she rejected. It's my image. That's all she's gotten to know. And I can hardly be responsible for what she chooses to see as my image."

Armed with such an attitude, inner-liberated persons feel free to take all kinds of risks in relationships that might intimidate others. They have little fear in sharing with others their good feelings about them. Yet others often are afraid to tell someone else, "I really like you." They fear being embarrassed if the other person didn't feel the same way about them. Inner-liberated persons have no such worry. They simply know what they themselves think and feel, and make no pretense to be responsible for what another person thinks and feels about them.

INFLUENCING OTHERS

The fact that you cannot expect to take responsibility for choosing someone else's thoughts in no way negates the possibility that you can have influence over what another person chooses to think. Certainly, you shouldn't berate yourself if your attempts to influence another are unsuccessful, since you have no control over another's thought choices. Above and beyond the conventional means that human beings employ to entice others to love them—persuasion, passionate appeals, appearance—one of the best techniques is to genuinely love them. That means of course that you deeply listen to and care for others on their own terms. Most of us are very much attracted to those who combine being lovable while also actively loving us.

A THOUGHT FOR YOUR FILES (CHOOSE ONE)

Defective Thought	Effective Thought
Oh, look how I stumbled upon this lovely place. I'm so *lucky.*	Oh, look how I stumbled upon this lovely place. *I* make nice things happen.

EASING UP

People act in some very strange ways in order to prove to themselves that they are worthy. Some go so far as to try to conquer others bodily and/or psychologically merely to prove to themselves that they have got "it." Some drive themselves relentlessly over others for positions of power. The irony, of course, is that they have been worthy of esteem all along. They were born with it, and it never left them. These anxious individuals just didn't stop long enough in their breathless pursuit of acceptance to appreciate what they have had in their possession ever since the day they were born. If only they were to pause to "center," to stop and think more effectively. When a person fully appreciates how acceptable he really is, an amazing thing begins to happen. He slows down. He stops running and panting. His life becomes mellow. He can find his center regularly. He no longer feels compelled to win all the prizes or conversely—to hide out and be afraid. He eases up and lets life in, instead of chasing around so desperately after it or running away from it. By coupling his lovability with openness, he makes an unbeatable combination, a combination that sustains his inner calm regardless of the external conditions that often confuse and upset others.

However, some cautions. It is unrealistic to think of yourself as totally lovable. Although you might be lovable under many conditions, there are still times when your environment can be unkind. Certainly it makes sense to treat yourself with at least the same amount of kindness and warmth you would offer to others, but is impractical to carry self love to an extreme. Narcissus, the extremely attractive youth described in Greek mythology, fell so in love with his own image that he literally starved while staring at his reflection in a pond—only to see it vanish each time he tried to kiss it. Certainly it is wise to listen to your own drummer, to care for your self deeply—but not to the exclusion of all others or everything else. Self-love need not be selfish!

Another reason why it is not a good idea to feel totally lovable is that you might become too complacent and smug. If you are not careful, you might end up just lying around eating grapes in what seems to be a Garden of Eden only to belatedly discover that this world is no longer a Garden of Eden; and undoubtedly, you'll run out of grapes and find that there's no one around to plant and tend a new crop for you. So then, let a little bit of creative anxiety slip into your life. Remind yourself that however lovable you are you are not totally lovable. That will serve to give you sufficient tension to get on with achieving the earthbound goals you will have set for yourself.

THE LOVABILITY CYCLE

As we've discussed, feeling realistically lovable, you will have a greater tendency to be loved. And when this feeling is projected, it generally proves to be most attractive to potential lovers. What is projected says in effect, "Look at me. I am easy to listen to deeply. I am easy to care for. I am easy to appreciate. Come share me with me."

And other persons tend to pick up on this message, to sense, "That is a person I want to listen to, to care for." And very often they do. Of course, we can fully appreciate that there is absolutely no guarantee that someone will cue in on our message of lovability. Yet, when someone does, a marvelous natural cycle begins—"the lovability cycle." You feel lovable, you tend to become loved, being loved confirms and reinforces the feeling of being lovable, and so on.

Effective Openness

Consider this: a criminal breaks into your house and, holding you at gunpoint, asks you the whereabouts of your valuables. Do you share with him openly all that he seeks? Even the fact that you have a wall safe that he knows nothing about. Probably not. To be totally open in such a circumstance could be quite stupid. It can be said, then, that to be effectively open means to be open to the proper degree, depending on the time, the circumstances, and the specific situation. Being effectively open is not nearly as obvious a proposition as it might at first glance seem.

Openness suggests being unguarded, self-revealing, honest. But to be effective, all of these qualities should be offered on a conditional basis only. I will not be unguarded, for example, in the company of bandits. In order for it to be effective openness, it is necessary that the openness be attained solely by choosing your own thoughts and that it not be predicated in any way upon what thoughts another chooses. In addition, the openness should be clearly possible, and it should enhance, not defeat, the purposes of inner liberation. All of the following discussion about effective openness implies that these criteria are met.

When you become effectively open, you will enjoy the freedom of being whoever you are, undisguised, transparent, with nothing to hide. By living so unpretentiously you will come to enjoy a deep level of inner calm, the first of the three essential dimensions of the inner-liberated person.

RESULTS OF BEING OPEN

Four advantages become yours as a result of being open. You don't have to remember what you say from one moment to the next, much less from one day to the other. People who deal with you deal with the real you, hence you learn the truth about how the real you is being received. Other people will tend to reciprocate and share their genuine selves with you, so that you will see the actual world of others rather than have to deal with a false picture. Finally, you will not have to bury your true feelings.

When I was a young man, I was prone to telling "whoppers." That is, I exaggerated quite a bit—a lot. Sometimes I would forget what I had told someone, and then I would slip up at a later date. When I was in the Navy, I knew someone who was even worse. He was a chronic liar. He would tell one story on Tuesday and then contradict himself on Thursday. He did this over and over again, and everyone at the base knew he was a liar. But this didn't seem to faze him. He just went on and on making up stories —stories to suit any occasion—and usually the stories had him as the hero. The reason most of us have exaggerated at some time or another in our lives is so that we might look a little better in the eyes of those we were trying to impress. It's only later in life that I found out that if I told the whole truth, as best I knew it, the world wouldn't fall out from under me; and there was the remarkable fringe benefit that I didn't have to remember what likes I had told in order to sustain the image I had created.

One time I lied to one of my best friends when I was in high school. In order to make myself look bigger in his eyes, I told him a highly exaggerated and detailed story about how I had seduced a girl we both admired. "Wow," he said, truly amazed at my seductive skills and sexual prowess. It was fully five years later that I, for some of the reasons we are discussing this very moment, decided to "go straight." "Don," I said, "you know that story I told you about five years ago?" "Yeah," he said, "how could I forget it?" "Don," I said, "it was all a damned lie." "Kush," he said, "how could you lie like that? You did it with such a straight face."

Of course I had trained myself to become an expert liar. The problem was that after a while, I had a great deal of difficulty in sorting out what was the truth about my life and what wasn't. I was losing track of the real me. But once I started telling the truth as much as possible, I found that not only did I not have to remember my stories, I didn't even have to remember what I said from moment to moment. If I contradict myself now, I am not even embarrassed, because I know that if I changed from moment to moment, it is not because I lied, but because I honestly perceive the situation differently now than I did even five minutes before.

Once you have become transparent, you have nothing left to hide. Many persons coming to therapy for the first time are extremely relieved to unburden themselves from their deep, dark secrets. They are sometimes quite surprised that the therapist isn't shocked or in despair, doesn't tell them to leave the office at once. Their lips tremble, their foreheads sweat, and their stomachs get tense as they relate this "terrible thing." But any seasoned therapist has learned to appreciate and be prepared to help with all modes of human behavior.

In my own case, I feel that I have very little that requires hiding. That is not to say that I would go around sporting my bank account on my sleeve or distribute photographs of my sex life. But if such facts became known, I believe that I would have no trouble whatsoever facing the world. I might not want to advertise my private affairs to my neighbors, but I am not very intimidated should anything that was true (or even untrue) about me become known.

I have learned that I am more than able to live a most satisfying inner life regardless of what others might think of me, especially those who don't care deeply for me. And those who really care for me, really listen to me on my own terms, are not going to be seriously misled by any untoward rumors and gossip, especially when they know me as being open with them. It's a fail-safe position.

It is easy, and often a pleasure, to be open with those who listen and care for me on my terms. And it is both a waste of time and next to impossible to be truly open with those who do not really listen to or care for what I have to say. These people, since they will not be hearing me in the way that I wish, are bound to misinterpret what I say—hearing, in a sense, only what they want to hear. This is a widespread and most natural phenomenon, one with which inner-liberated persons have come to terms.

One of the ways to get in touch with your own strengths and weaknesses is to be as honest with yourself as possible (with one notable exception, which we will discuss shortly). And interestingly enough, one of the best ways to be honest with yourself is to be authentic and honest in your dealings with others. Then, as they reflect back to you how they are perceiving you, you will learn something substantive about yourself.

Supposing, for example, that you were pretending to be my friend, and you said you enjoyed my company when in actuality you felt just the opposite. Would I be learning anything worthwhile about either you or me? Would I in fact be responding to the real you or merely a characterization of you? If I don't deal with the real you, then as I relate back to your false image, it is not really you to whom I am relating! Therefore, in our transactions, both of us are bound to learn absolutely nothing accurate about each other. What an empty pursuit, especially if one of your goals in life includes the pursuit of accurate, realistic self-knowledge. By such dishonesty a person could actually sabotage his own chances of realizing a life goal of major significance—accurate self-knowledge. Individuals who are chronically dishonest are not very worthwhile associates. If, for example, you were to surround yourself with "yes men," it would be extremely difficult for you to find out the truth in a given situation.

Unfortunately, there are many people who allow themselves to become surrounded by these inauthentic types and often find that they themselves are sometimes acting in the very same way. Usually this starts as a form of self-defense and later becomes a habit. So beware of "phonies," and avoid them as much as possible lest you become one yourself.

Yvonne, a twenty-seven-year-old schoolteacher, came to see me, seeking help after losing much of her confidence in judging other people's integrity. "I don't trust my own judgment anymore," she said, "particularly when it comes to men."

Yvonne had married someone only to discover that he was entirely different than she had expected him to be. "Tom, when we were dating, seemed so reliable, so considerate. Then after we were married, he turned out to be just the opposite. He couldn't keep a job, and I never knew whether to believe him or not. He lied about everything. I even found out that he was married before and had a child from that marriage. He never told me about it." As a result, Yvonne naturally became overly suspicious about almost everything. "I'm not the open, naive little girl that I used to be," she said bitterly during an early counseling session. As a result of counseling, in which she learned about and experimented with the concept of *effective openness,* she began to develop a more sophisticated and realistic understanding of when to trust and when not to trust. It is extremely important that a person not become so embittered by another's dishonesty that she does not permit herself the privilege of continuing to be intelligently trusting.

Authenticity, just like inauthenticity, is catching. If I am open and honest with you, then it is a good bet that you will be open and honest with me. Therefore, if I want to expand my life space, know more about the people who live in this world, it pays off, and pays off handily, to be open and honest.

Elton, a young executive and a client of mine, was concerned about his lack of warm friendships, especially at work. At one point he complained, however, that he could see no reason he should share any part of his personal life with Frank, his colleague. "Frank never confided anything about himself to me, so why should I do otherwise?" But then one day over lunch, according to Elton's story, Frank asked for help. "I'm in very big trouble here at the office. The company is moving across town, and I told the boss that I want no part in that decision. He's been on my tail ever since. Calling me disloyal and everything." Elton said he didn't know how to interpret Frank's sudden rush of confidence and trust in him. They had never shared confidences before. "Why should we now?" Elton preferred to be suspicious of Frank's "angle."

Obviously, the relationship between Elton and Frank was

one of convenience rather than depth. Yet if Frank was being open and honest and was authentically sharing part of himself to Elton, it is unfortunate that his effort was not being fully appreciated. Elton eventually learned how to risk "caring," and in the process he opened the door to a more genuine relationship with others. Generally, if it is not highly out of character, as it was in the above instance, your being open can encourage those with whom you have shared something to be open with you. However, once you gain a reputation for being closed, like Frank, it generally takes others some time before they will trust you sufficiently to take you fully into their confidence.

Sometimes in group-counseling sessions, someone will take what for him is a very big risk and share something that is extremely important and personal to him. During such sessions, I urge that all members make it their business to attempt to listen deeply and care whenever others try to share authentically. Invariably I have noticed that when one person does take such a risk, in a short while a number of others also come forth and risk similarly. Such behavior is contagious.

On the few occasions when one person shared something about himself that was deeply personal and the others did not really listen and care but instead sat in judgment, offered critical comments, or worse still, disregarded entirely what was said, the person who was sharing tended to clam up, and as a result of this offense most of the subsequent offerings of group members were quite superficial.

There are various levels of communication. On the surface is the small talk—talk about the weather, talk about what is perfectly obvious. On another level is communication where information is known to one party but not to the other, information as innocuous as "You have lipstick on your teeth," or as sensitive as "My marriage is breaking up." It is the sharing of sensitive and personal material that reveals whether you are truly open. Of course, some kinds of sensitive material should not be shared with just anyone. But in general, inner-liberated persons find that they have very little about themselves that they feel compelled to keep under wraps. What gives them the most difficulty is the discriminate handling of other people's secrets, since they prefer in general not to know unnecessarily sensitive data about another.

A THOUGHT FOR YOUR FILES (CHOOSE ONE)

Defective Thought	Effective Thought
I think that if people ever found out what I'm really like, my world would fall apart. I'm a very private person.	I enjoy my privacy. But frankly, I don't mind sharing any aspect of myself whatsoever providing, of course, the inquirer really cares about me.

The advantages of being open far outweigh the disadvantages, but as I've stated, there are several limitations involved in baring your soul too openly.

Everything is relative, including most of the so-called "truths" we've come to know. In fact, things are changing so fast that one social scientist, Gilbert Wrenn, recommends that every day we should unlearn one so-called fact that we mistakenly think is true. Obviously, the truth is elusive at best—even if we were to be totally committed to sharing it in perfectly open fashion in a given instance. For example, suppose a good friend of yours requests, "Please tell me how you honestly feel toward me." Such an inquiry may be more dangerous and difficult than you might imagine. Even if you fully intend to respond in total honesty, you might find it extremely difficult. This is because words often obfuscate rather than clarify. The word is merely the symbol for the "thing," and not the thing itself. Exceptions that come from our mouths are sighs, yells, and whistles—which are the "thing" itself and not mere symbols. But since

most words are but symbols, we must settle only for ap-
proximations of the actual. Therefore, if you were to
seriously attempt to put into words exactly how you feel,
you would be doomed to fall short.

Hermann Hesse, wrote in *Siddhartha:* "Words do not
express thoughts very well; everything immediately
becomes a little different, a little distorted, a little foolish.
And yet, it also pleases me and seems right that what is of
value and wisdom to one man seems nonsense to another."

However, we can communicate in ways that go beyond
words. Our body language often speaks clearly. Unfortunately, we have seriously curtailed the use of various
kinds of touching that can be used to convey warmth
and care. In the American culture, touching another
person, except in *very* conventional ways—handshakes,
pats on the back, etc.—is hardly permitted. Touch in a
less than conventional way is often misconstrued as an
act of aggression or sexual assault. There are very few
shades of gray permitted. This seriously impairs our
ability to communicate ordinary warmth and affection
for another through touch.

So then if your friend does request that you share
your honest feelings about him, you will be doing so ad-
visedly. The best you can offer any person is a severely
edited version of all the thoughts that have passed
through your mind. Whenever we are moved to speak,
only a small percentage of what goes through our minds
is channeled into voice. In fact, sometimes we lie as
much or more by omission than by commission. Have
you ever seen another person cheat at something and
still not turned them in? If so, don't be alarmed. It's
cultural ethic. There is an unwritten code in this culture
that it is ungentlemanly, even treacherous, to report another's crime. Yet, is this silence not lying by omission?
Of course it is. Inner-liberated persons fully appreciate
this and hence do not permit themselves to feel too self-
righteous about their true level of honesty. In fact, as

you will see, inner-liberated persons are not very self-righteous about many things at all.

It is important for you to realize that you cannot possibly be totally honest. There are occasions when you will not speak because you do not want to unnecessarily hurt another person's feelings. At other times you will remain silent because you realize that your words will only be misunderstood. You will sometimes remain silent because you cannot find the words to say at a given moment. There will be many occasions when it will be too late to speak your mind.

Supposing you were able to tell this hypothetical friend of yours exactly how you did feel about him. Even if you were able to find the "perfect" words to describe your feelings toward him, it is still possible that you would be misunderstood. Through a process known as selective perception, all of us tend to hear largely what we want to hear rather than exactly what was said. Selective perception is a natural and common phenomenon.

I once gave a talk to a group of parents about family counseling. A parent came up to me after my talk and said, "Dr. Kushel, I couldn't agree more with what you said. It is about time someone said—(whatever it is that she wanted to hear)." She proceeded to tell me, idea by idea, what she heard me say in my talk. Frankly, I would have not recognized one word of what she said as my own if she hadn't told me that it was what I had said. Obviously, she heard me say only what she wanted to hear me say.

In addition to being misunderstood by your friend, it is also possible that he never really wanted you to share your feelings about him, even though he said just that. Merely because someone asks you for your opinion does not necessarily mean that they really want it. People often request "honest feedback" from each other—only to resent tremendously the fact that they received just what they asked for.

CREATIVE SELF-DECEPTION

Although as a general rule inner-liberated persons go to great lengths to be absolutely truthful with themselves, priding themselves on their ability to face the facts and do something about them, there is one notable exception to this rule: Whenever reality is so horrid or immutable that there is no *harm* done by temporarily deceiving themselves, they do so.

For example, as in the case of Viktor Frankl, temporary self-deception permitted him to survive a Nazi concentration camp. He looked for positives in that horrible situation, and he found them. But he did not continue to delude himself once he was released. However, while there, he chose effective (though sometimes self-deceptive) thoughts rather that necessarily "right" thoughts.

Imagine for a moment that you have been imprisoned unjustly, convicted without right of appeal, as was Frankl, and you knew you would not be free for a long time, if ever. Would it be imprudent to delude yourself that you were, indeed, having something "worthwhile" happening to you, regardless of how awful it really was by any objective standards? Of course not. You always owe it to yourself to make the best of what is a pretty bad situation, and if creative, pragmatic self-deception helps, then by all means use it— as long as no one else is injured by your view. Creative use of temporary self-deception, as part of the autosuggestion technique that we explored previously, can be employed to help you lose weight, stop smoking, improve your sex life, and in countless other situations where you use it to help yourself and not to harm anyone else.

There are two necessary conditions that need emphasis, though, before you permit yourself to be deceived: the assurance that no one is going to be hurt, and that you can return to objective reality at will.

If a person hears his child calling for help and he realizes that his youngster is playing along a dangerous river bank, there is no question that he would not want to deceive himself. On the other hand, if the child is playing safely in a playpen and the father checked and double-checked to see that everything is in good order, he might do well not to hear his youngster occasionally. Supposing that this particular child is in the habit of throwing tantrums and that such tantrums and screams are ritualistic ways of getting attention. In this instance, I think you will agree, the imaginative use of self-deception might very well be a blessing.

If a person has a heart condition, it most certainly would be inappropriate for him to delude himself that he need not take necessary precautions about smoking or overeating. Yet, of course, many persons practice this kind of dangerous self-deception every day. This kind of self-deception is not very creative.

You must delude yourself only on a purposeful and temporary basis. You must make certain before you enter into any deceptive bargain with yourself that you can bring yourself back to reality—at will. If, as in the previous example, you were committed to two years in a hell hole with no hope of escape or reprieve, it would be in your self-interest to delude yourself. However, it would be very important that you returned to reality once you were released.

It is important that you be as honest with *yourself* as you can possibly be (allowing for the fact that creative self-deception is fully under your control and always a temporary arrangement). If you permit yourself to believe what others say about you (good and bad), you easily lose sight of who you are. Understanding certain truths about yourself, difficult as they may be to face, will lead to further growth and development. Inappropriate self-deception can prevent you from this personal growth. If you continue to believe that you are a .300 hitter in baseball but your actual batting average is only .180, self-deception might keep you from improving your hitting stance. If you were to deceive yourself that your marriage is fine when in reality it is disintegrating, that would be foolish since such deception could prevent you from improving the situation while there was still time.

So then, having reviewed most of the important misconceptions about openness, let us return to the old cliché and, with our new perspectives, employ it! "Honesty is always the best policy."

A THOUGHT FOR YOUR FILES (CHOOSE ONE)

Defective Thought

I am totally open.

Effective Thought

I am effectively open.

THE THREE CALMING QUESTIONS

Inner-liberated persons frequently ask themselves three important questions—and they find the answer to each of them extremely conducive to calm. As we move along, you will increasingly understand why. The three calming questions are:

What time is it? (The answer is always "now.")

Where am I? (The answer is always "here.")

Who is that person I am with? (The answer is always "me.")

Why the answers are so calming is perhaps obvious to you already. Inner-liberated persons have learned the secret of how to make every "now" and "here" just as satisfying as possible. And since they've learned to really value being with themselves, it is no wonder that they feel reassured.

THE OPENNESS CYCLE

Just as with the lovability cycle, there is the openness cycle. It, too, is self-reinforcing and works like this: tell the truth (effectively) and you are responded to in kind, making it even easier to continue to be effectively open.

Chapter
·6·
STEP FIVE:
Clarifying Purpose

When you take a photograph at the beach, there can be so many worthy subjects and scenes that it's difficult to know just where to aim your camera. Yet the most significant pictures are those that are *focused,* that have a specific subject, that make a statement, that make order out of this random detail. Perhaps you choose to focus your lens on that child playing by the shoreline or on those splashing waves beyond, on the gull swooping in gracefully, low over the water. But to your immediate left is a fascinating picture too. The lifeguards holding court with young ladies. Why doesn't it work when you do it all at once?

Have you ever been subjected to a friend's home movies, movies that panned all over the place, that tried to take in everything all at once? "See, that is St. Mark's Square. Did you see that? That was the Pitti Palace that flashed by. Oh, the Bell Tower. Look, that was Shirley waving." At the end you had a bad case of Excedrin headache and could remember little of consequence. Would it not have been better if your friend had decided on a single subject? At least then there might have been a focus, a center point. With priority and purpose he would have established a qualitative rather than a quantitive interest.

A very satisfying personal existence is, of course, the primary aim of an inner-liberated person. He assumes that life is here not simply to be endured, but to be enjoyed as much as possible. Still, "enjoyment" and "satisfaction" vary considerably from individual to individual.

Often there is greater pleasure in the anticipation of pleasure rather than in the pleasure itself. The popular song title, "Is That All There Is?" reflects the disappointment often experienced when a long sought after but relatively empty goal was finally realized. Life is a process rather than an end in itself, a journey rather than merely a destination. Since it is your mission to enjoy that journey, the goals that you set for yourself should be designed to add to the quality of the journey. Although it is possible that your deepest goals might never be realized, the journey definitely should be.

TURNING PROBLEMS INTO PROJECTS

Is there not sometimes pleasure in a hard day's work—especially if the work is connected with something that has special meaning to you? There can be tremendous pleasure in successfully tackling problems and turning them into challenging projects. In fact, it can be safely stated that inner-liberated persons have no real *problems,* only *projects.* The difference is that a problem just sits there untackled whereas to have a project means that a plan, a strategy for dealing with the former problem, has been formulated and is in process.

PASSIONATE PURPOSE

Colin Fletcher, in *The Man Who Walked Through Time,* writes about his decision to walk through the Grand Canyon:

I saw that my decision to walk through the Canyon could mean more than I knew. I saw that by going down into that huge fissure in the face of the earth, deep into the space and the silence and the solitude, I might come as close as we can at present to moving back and down through the smooth and apparently impenetrable face of time. If I could contribute enough, the journey might teach me in the end, with a certainty no book can give, how the centuries have built the world we know. For I would see how the rocks had been constructed, and how they had been carved. How life had mushroomed from simple beginnings into the complex and astonishing pageant we now accept so casually. How it had covered the rocks with a web whose intricate and interlocking structure all too often becomes invisible to us "civilized" and estranged people. I would see many strands from the web . . .

The easiest route may not be the most pleasurable, the most satisfying route. To view the Grand Canyon from its rim is awe-inspiring. But you need only your visual senses to view it. It is a more enriching experience to walk directly into it—to experience the canyon with your whole body, with all of your senses. More is required of you, but more is returned to you as well. The willingness to endure the hardships of such a walk (up the canyon as well as down) obviously requires a clarity and passion of purpose.

It is our *passionate* personal purposes that give us the zest and energy to take on the tough challenges that give momentum and direction to our lives.

It is your purposes that help you transcend yourself. When you reach slightly beyond your capacity, you often muster the energy to excel—to exceed your imagined capacity. Reaching out to share with others, to help another, to love another, is, for many, a major purpose for living. To reach out to those less fortunate than you is usually interpreted an act of altruism, but it is self-serving as well. Dr. Hans Selye, the noted authority on stress, calls this kind of service to others "self-serving altruism" because the pleasure one receives from such an activity often adds more to the inner quality of the helper than it does the person who was helped.

Helping others, your fellow man, is always viewed as virtuous whereas helping yourself is often viewed as a selfish, even "thoughtless," act. But inner-liberated persons don't rely very much on others helping them, preferring, as much as possible, to be self-reliant. They are especially self-reliant when it comes to choosing thoughts about altruism. They generally do engage in many acts that superficially appear totally altruistic—caring for a sick friend, giving generously to a charity, helping a neighbor move furniture in, loving others in inner-liberating fashion, and listening to and caring for others on their own terms. But the truth is that these seemingly pure altruistic acts are in reality quite self-serving. If they weren't, these persons wouldn't be doing them. After all, they are determined to have the most satisfying inner life that is humanly possible.

They gain by giving in at least one of three ways: they receive an inner pleasure from the act of giving ("I felt good sharing. His smile reminded me of my father's," etc.); they actually enjoy the activity for its own sake ("Moving his furniture was tough, but I really needed and enjoyed the exercise."); the act of giving helps them transcend themselves for a time ("I stopped doting on my own situation for a while.") It may also be that "being generous" is one of the special purposes of life that the giver has decided upon for himself.

A benign, sometimes altruistic, hedonism is an inner-liberating characteristic: self-sacrifice certainly is not.

PURPOSES: LOVING AND ACHIEVING

I asked the adult students in one of the graduate classes I teach to list their significant life goals. Their goals fell into two distinct categories—loving others, and achieving. Under the category of "loving others" were such subgoals as "seeing my children secure and happy" and "developing and sustaining a deep and intimate relationship with someone special." The achieving category included such desires as "completing my education," "traveling and seeing (a special place or places)," "becoming successful in my chosen career," "writing," "building," "completing (a special project of some type)."

In your own way, have you established clearly in your mind, your own life's purpose? Are your purposes absolutely clear to you? Are you passionate or merely casual about these purposes?

Inner-liberated persons establish purposes for themselves that are very personal, clear—and passionate.

These purposes are not to be confused with the pastimes that often give only a temporary illusion of meaning—such as "more college credits," "a movie that I must see," "a weekend trip we are planning," "the living room I must get redecorated," or "Mah-Jongg on Wednesday." Not that these pastimes are without value. They do serve to pass time—if that is all that you want to do. But inner-liberating purposes are not mere pastimes.

How are these significant purposes to be located? How can such purposes be clarified if indeed they are so necessary for inner liberation?

Clarifying Passionate Purposes

There are two major obstacles that can stand in the way of clarifying your passionate purposes: loneliness anxiety, and the illusion that the pursuit of more money is a valid end in itself. Only after you have jumped these two hurdles will you be free to truly begin the clarification process. Let's attack the loneliness-anxiety obstacle first.

THE FEAR OF LONELINESS

Many people have never come to terms with their existential loneliness. If you have never come to fully understand what it is to be totally alone, devastatingly alone, and have not worked-through this fundamental aspect of life, you will be forever kept from finding your genuine purposes in life.

It is not necessary that you actively go out and seek loneliness in order to overcome loneliness anxiety. All you need do is to let some of it into your life, to accept lonely moments rather than try to deny their existence by keeping artificially busy. After all, there's plenty of loneliness around, and to permit yourself some of it, to let some of seep into your life, is no crime. In fact, allowing sufficient doses of loneliness in is a most human enterprise. When you do so, you are actively engaging in one of the universal qualities experienced by man. You will be, paradoxically, in plenty of good company.

You must have experienced some degree of loneliness at one time in your life. If you haven't acknowledged this, you are depriving yourself of one of the most important ingredients of the human experience. Of course, being deeply and devastatingly alone is no fun. For most of us it is terribly frightening.

I'm not referring to a time when you felt a little bit neglected or hurt. I mean times in your life when you felt totally misunderstood, very much uncared for, quite unloved and unappreciated, abandoned by someone who really mattered. You can be just as lonely in a room crowded with people—even with family, colleagues, and friends—as you can be on a deserted island. When truly lonely, you feel totally isolated and cut off.

This experience can be so unpleasant, so frightening in fact, that many people have vowed never to let anything like that happen to them again. According to Clarke Moustakis, in his book *Loneliness:*

It is the terror of loneliness, not loneliness itself, but loneliness anxiety, the fear of being left alone, of being left out that most persons resist. . . . It is absolutely necessary to keep busy, active, have a full schedule, be with others, escape into fantasies, dramas, and lives of others on television or in the movies. Everything is geared toward filling and killing time to avoid feeling the emptiness in life and the vague dissatisfactions of acquiring possessions, gaining status and power, and behaving in appropriate and approved ways. The escape from loneliness is actually an escape from the fear of loneliness.

Many deny the existence of loneliness and run from it. This running from reality (by aimless movement, temporary escapes), this denial, keeps us from coming to grips with and eventually accepting the fact that we are alone in this world. Yet, once we accept loneliness as is, we can slow down, stop running, ease up on our busyness, stop fearing—and begin to live, to relate, and most importantly, to discover our genuine, rather than our fleeting purposes.

A THOUGHT FOR YOUR FILES (CHOOSE ONE)

Defective Thought	Effective Thought
I can't stand being alone. I need others very often. If I'm alone too long, I get very sad. I get lonely. I must keep busy.	I often enjoy being alone these days. I've come to terms with it. I have learned to be very much alone without being lonely. I do not fear or run from loneliness even when it sometimes comes.

David Riesman, in his classic *The Lonely Crowd,* writes:

Literally, millions of adults who are protected and loved, who experienced intimate relations in their early years, suffer the consequences of an impersonal, competitive world of self-denial and alienation. They often go to great lengths to escape or overcome the fear of loneliness, to avoid any direct or genuine facing of their own inner experience. What is it that drives man to surround himself with the external double-talk, the same surface interests and activities during his evenings at home as during his days at work?

A client of mine whose wife suddenly abandoned him and their three children and went off with another man was unprepared for the loneliness that inevitably ensued. "I could not imagine being so alone. Our life, I thought, was based on mutuality—on love and commitment. I was totally unprepared." He had never come to terms, it seems, in advance of his abandonment, with this fundamental fact of life.

Human ties through loneliness

Moustakis writes:

> Strange as it may seem, the individual, in being lonely, if let be, will realize himself in loneliness and create a bond or sense of fundamental relatedness with others. Loneliness rather than separating the individual or causing a break or division of self, expands the individual's wholeness, perceptiveness, sensitivity, and humanity. It enables the person to realize human ties and awareness hitherto unknown.

It is only when you begin to fully comprehend this fact of life that you will be able to see the sun come up tomorrow in a totally new way. You will begin to experience your own unique inner feelings, the insides of your body, more sensually, more vitally, than you have ever experienced them before. It is alone that the most profound experiences in life can be appreciated and subsequently shared. Moments of intense suffering, loss, pain. These can ultimately be shared with another as part of a communal loneliness. Certainly in the creative experience, there is often no other way but the lonely way, as most serious artists will testify.

Fully accepting the fact of your loneliness leads to the state where, although you may not delight over the reality that you are essentially alone in this world, you realize that at least you can live with it. There is, naturally, a certain melancholy connected with the acceptance of this fact of life. It is through a veil of melancholy that you face life as it is—not as you might have dreamed, or wished it to be.

From this deep awareness of your fundamental alone-ness, you are moved to ask with *passion: "Why* life? Why my *life?* What is it that I genuinely, all *alone,* want from this, my life?" Suddenly you discover that you *must* find an answer if you are to go on. So you pursue the questions as to what you are about and what it is that you want out of this, your life, with a renewed vigor.

MONEY

The second obstacle standing in the way of your clarifica-tion of purpose is the relentless pursuit of money. Money, of course, is power. But if you have plenty of personal power, as you will once you become fully inner-liberated, money will become proportionately less important to you. Still, as the late comedian Joe E. Lewis once said, "It doesn't matter whether you are rich or poor, it is still nice to have money." Inner-liberated persons are not known for throwing their money away, but they are also not known for letting the passionate pursuit of dollars spoil the quality of their inner lives. They strive not for money per se but for exciting goals that may incidentally have a sound financial payoff and will absolutely have a personal payoff.

If you are like most people, you are interested in a num-ber of material possessions—a nice home, a reliable auto-mobile (perhaps two), money for an extended vacation now and then, a few luxuries, sending the kids to college, and security for retirement. There is little question that money occupies the thoughts of most people, and it undoubtedly preoccupies the thought track of those who do not have enough much more than those who do. Unfortunately, very few people feel that they have enough, even the very, very rich.

A THOUGHT FOR YOUR FILES (CHOOSE ONE)

Defective Thought	Effective Thought
I enjoy and feel proud that I own my own home, this gorgeous coat, this brooch, this business firm. I know there are many people who are jealous of me and would like to take them away. I'm keeping my eye on these things that I own, to protect them.	I travel light. I sometimes enjoy using extravagant things. Although I possess legal title to a number of material objects, I don't feel that I "own" them. I think of the "use" of things, and I realize that my use of them is strictly *pro tem*. After all, I don't want these "things" to restrict my flexibility and spontaneity. When I'm away from them, let anyone else use them. The way I look at it, every material possession I have is merely "rented," not owned, and I like it that way. I'm not going to be buried with things, I'll leave that to King Tut.

How much money is enough? This, of course, is a very personal question. For some there is little comfort in knowing that two-thirds of the world's people go to bed hungry every night when they "need" and don't have sufficient cash for what might seem a luxury to another—a new suit or dress, theater tickets, or even air fare to visit one's far-off sick parent. The issue of *enough* is relative, and is more a matter of attitude than reality. Since *enough* is an attitude, inner-liberated persons simply choose the most effective attitude possible about *enough* money and work it from there.

Too many persons spend an inordinate amount of their limited time preoccupied with "How can I make more?" "How can I save more?" "How can I win (or even steal) more?" Certainly these are very human questions, questions about *enough*. Following is an illustration of a sound line of thought taken by inner-liberated persons about this very sensitive issue:

"Money. I like it. It's great. Money is power, and I most certainly need some of it to attain the basic necessities of life: food, shelter, clothing. Fortunately, my family and I have enough for at least the basic necessities, otherwise I'd have to think of some ways to earn more of the stuff. However, there are two ways to get really rich. One way is to make lots of money—that's the hard way. The other way is to change my attitude about it—that's the easy way, the inner-liberated way.

"There is one basic necessity that no amount of money can buy. Effective ideas. Effective thoughts. Luckily, these ideas are free, and I've stored up a batch of them—from people I have gotten to know, from the public library, from thinking through certain principles all on my own. And it's these essential ideas that have given me so much personal power, so any additional power that accrues to me in the form of money is not of major consequence. It's not that I can't enjoy money and what it can buy, it's just that the heavy pursuit of it is not very high on my list of personal priorities as long as I have enough for the basics.

"It might be nice to have some additional power and influence. But it is hardly very essential—to my way of thinking. Hardly worth pursuing madly, the way so many people seem to be doing.

"If, by chance, I were to suddenly inherit a large fortune, win the sweepstakes, or something like that, my way of life would not change in any significant way. I would still continue having *my* very satisfying personal existence, the same high-quality inner existence that I currently enjoy. I would still continue to engage with vitality each day as it comes—moment by moment—choosing effective thoughts as needed, independently, qualitatively enjoying myself and my life.

"I would still continue to be personally successful regardless of surroundings. I would still jump out of bed in the morning with my own energy, open my own eyes to enjoy the day, put my own two feet on the floor, and splash water on the very same face—rich or poor. And when I looked in the mirror, I would still see me. There's just no getting away from 'me.' Wherever I go, I'm always there.

"I'd still have my one and only body. The very same mind. I would still be taking good care of the only two things I really own in this world, my body and my mind. And I take very good care of both of these possessions now —and I would, in the very same way, if I were wealthy. To jog in the morning still takes only me and my feet. It's my circulatory system. My heart and lungs don't know the meaning of excessive cash.

"Nothing of significance about the quality of my inner life, my real life, could possibly change through acquiring a lot of money. Choosing an effective thought doesn't require even a nickel. No matter what the situation, it will still be I who have to do the intelligent choosing.

"And if I ask myself the three calming questions, I still will have the same answers. 'What time is it?' *Now.* 'Where are you?' *Here.* And, 'Who is that person that you are with?' *Me.* And since I have found the the answers extremely reassuring, since the 'me' that I'm invariably with is definitely a good fellow to be around, life with millions of dollars couldn't be any better. The making of a lot of money just isn't involved in the answer to any of these three most basic of all questions.

"What about money for my loved ones, my dependents, you ask? Well, of course they need the necessities too. And I'm sure that extra money for their clothing, college, travel, and a few luxuries will be welcome. But what I really offer to those I love is much more significant than money. I feel that what I share with them is much more lasting and of much greater value than anything money can buy.

"I offer them the opportunity to find a truly satisfying inner existence for themselves. The best way I can do this is by being that way and enjoying that kind of life for myself, everyday, and then hope that some of what I have learned and the way I live will wash off to some extent on them. No guarantee of course. But there is a good chance. Certainly, living my life this way is better than lecturing to my loved ones on how they might also live better. An inner-liberated lifestyle is best *caught,* rather than taught."

Once you develop this reasonable perspective toward the making of money, you can concentrate on more significant purposes for yourself.

YOUR PURPOSE IS INCOMPARABLE

Now that you have learned to avoid the obstacles of loneliness anxiety and the issue of enough money, you are ready to clarify for yourself your own passionate purposes— whether they include loving certain others, creating certain works, accomplishing particular projects, or achieving special experiences. It is the *pursuit* in and of itself that will give your life greatest meaning. You will not have to compare yourself to Beethoven to compose the music of your purposes. Or paint like Goya. Or design like Frank Lloyd Wright, for that matter. What you choose to accomplish is up to you, and it will be up to you to establish whatever standards you wish.

For example, if you decide that one of your prime purposes is to plant and grow the best tomatoes you have ever planted and grown in your life, it will be up to you to decide if you have met your objective. All that is required for an inner-liberating purpose is that it be genuine (that is, of your own choosing) and that it be a passionate pursuit (arriving out of your own sense of aloneness). Your purpose is yours alone and hence is *incomparable.*

As you may recall, at the outset I described how lonely I felt when the Dean's Search Committee rejected my candidacy at the college where I work. It was through that very experience that I was able to clarify for myself one of the most exciting purposes for living that I have ever had. After a period of dejection and anger, it suddenly struck me that I had always wanted to be an artist but that I had forgotten about that wish for many years. The events and challenges of earning a living sometimes take us far afield from the goals and dreams that we once had as children. For years and years, I had forgotten that I had at one time very seriously wanted to be an artist.

While on sabbatical, my wife, children, and I stopped with our trailer for a few days at a small Mexican town, San Miguel de Allende. I enrolled in a painting class for a few days at the local institute. One day I emerged with a portrait I had done of an old Mexican woman. "Jerry," my wife, Selma, said, "you're very good. Why don't you become a serious painter?" Her words hit me with surprising impact.

I enrolled as a freshman in college, apprenticed myself to an accomplished artist, studied independently for a number of years, and I have become a serious student of art! I consider (to myself) that I am becoming a significant painter. With my art work, it is not very important to me what others might think. "Becoming a significant painter" is too personal a goal, too passionate a goal, for me to put myself under the control of others' judgment. Over the years now, I have had some exhibitions in professional galleries, and as it happens, my work has sold. But what others think of it is not all that important to me, partly, I realize, because I don't have to rely upon the selling of my art to eat, and partly because the painting I do is to satisfy mainly "me," and me "alone." I have found in both the act of painting and the results of painting a deep sense of communion with something larger than myself. It has something to do, I believe, with the magical ways that colors interact on canvas. Painting is, to me, something of a metaphysical, religious experience.

Finding the purpose of "becoming a significant painter" has added to my life in numerous ways. For one thing, I really want to feel "very special and unique," and the fact that I am an artist satisfies that deeply felt want. Since I *create* my paintings, no one else can do them quite like me. I am irreplaceable when it comes to completing the works I have in mind. This makes me feel very special indeed.

It is because I needed to feel special, I believe, that I strove so desperately earlier in my life—to "earn" honorable posts on my job. Now, that scenario continues, but this time under my full control.

In addition, the purpose of "becoming a significant painter" has made my day-to-day life infinitely easier in many different ways. No longer do I feel pressed to excel as a therapist, a teacher, or much else. The pressure is off. Paradoxically, even though I tend to try less as a therapist and a teacher, my clients and students have indicated that my services are at least as effective as before, if not more so.

"But you were lucky. You had a natural talent," I've been told. However, I don't believe that talent had very much, if anything, to do with this. First I clarified my passionate purpose, largely by overcoming the obstacle of loneliness anxiety. Then I went out and *developed* the talent required to achieve this particular purpose of mine. Not the other way around. If you find a great enough *purpose,* somehow you will make it your business to do whatever is necessary to achieve your ends.

Living off the street. A few years ago I was in San Francisco to attend a professional conference. Ordinarily, I would have busied myself at the convention by walking around wearing my name card, my identity firmly pinned to my chest for all to see. Dr. Gerald Kushel, Professor, C. W. Post Center, Long Island University. But suddenly I had a strong sensation of *déja vu.* What was I doing "again" at one of these conventions? The same kinds of faces, the same panels, talks, ideas, new form perhaps, but mostly old, old ideas with new trappings.

So out in the streets I went, back to my hotel, and into comfortable clothes. I purchased a set of soft pastels and some quality rag paper and went about the city seeing, sensing, and *painting.* A couple of days later, when I had finished three paintings, I took them down to Fisherman's Wharf to see if I could sell them (since they would be difficult to carry home and also because they might have special sales appeal for their local scenery).

Next to a bagpipe player stood a woman who was hoping to sell her painted pictures of flowers. "Would you mind displaying and perhaps selling my three pictures at your stall?" I asked.

"I can't do that," she said. "I may not be here all that long. But why don't you set up here, between me and that bagpipe player? There's still plenty of room along the curb."

"But I don't have a license." I said. "Don't you need a license?"

"What are you worried about?" she said. "I have met some of the most wonderful people I have ever known in jail."

My heart beat fast, but I set up my three paintings on the curb and sat down next to them on the curb. People, many people, walked by. Some children stopped and looked. "Did you do that, man?" one young boy asked.

"Yes," I said proudly.

"Pretty good," he said. "If I had any money I'd buy it." Then he skipped off with his friends. But later, good fortune struck and I sold one of my works. It was a very earthy experience. Very exciting. A very direct experience—one that I had never tasted before.

After a while, as I was packing up my two remaining paintings and preparing to leave, the woman who was selling the flower paintings came over. Apparently she was very intuitive. "I know what you are doing here," she said. "You do? "What is it?" "You're trying to find out if you can live off the street," she said without blinking.

It stands to reason, does it not, that if you have established for yourself a genuine purpose (painting, writing, poetry, researching something that is of special interest to you, even observing the interaction of others, studying the geography of a region, making quality shoes, studying architectural design, or whatever), you can move authentically and gracefully through many a place and situation that you would not even consider if you had no sense of larger purposes.

Loving Others

Although in some ways you are very much alone, you still have a need to be affiliated, to be in touch with others. Choosing thoughts that enable you to come close to another, to listen to and care for another, is well within your capacity. And when you feel truly connected, even if it is with only one other person, your life takes on meaning and purpose.

Effectively loving another in inner-liberating fashion requires understanding and putting into practice several important concepts: nonpossessiveness, I-thou parity, and personal openness.

NONPOSSESSIVENESS

When an inner-liberated person chooses thoughts that offer love to another, the love offered is *nonpossessive*. That is, a warm and caring quality is offered, but it is offered without making any demands whatsoever upon the party to whom it is offered. "If I choose to love you, it does not mean that I choose to own you or, for that matter, to take responsibility for you." Inner-liberated persons offer the same kind of love to others that they would have for themselves. They, too, are not apt to be possessed or owned by another. Regardless of appearances, they remain thoroughly autonomous and free. When they love another, they care for them, appreciate them as best they can, for what they "are," not for what they "wish" they were. Inner-liberated love requires that you not try to make the person you love over in any way; nor are you permitted to feel that because you love this other person you *own* him. A person is not a house, a ring, or chattel. The truth is that you never really own anything in this world but your *own* body, and your *own* mind; and you most certainly never own someone else's.

Therefore, the love you offer this other person is characterized by a nonpossessive warmth, a warmth that says, in essence, "I care for you. I value you. I love you. I am available to listen and to care for you on your own terms, if you wish. However, I do not own you, and appreciate that you do not have to feel loving toward me in order for me to feel loving toward you." Again, the inner-liberated person reminds himself, "I have a full-time job taking responsibility for my own thoughts, feelings, and behavior, and I do not have any control whatsoever over the thoughts and feelings that another person chooses."

Harrington, a thirty-five-year-old graduate student and a client of mine, was depressed because the girl he loved, Paulette, did not return his passions. "She's the most wonderful person I have ever known," he said. "I can't stop thinking about her day or night. I wish I could, but I can't. I've never adored anyone as much as I do Paulette, and I can't bear the thought that she might be talking or even paying attention to another man. Even the thought of it drives me crazy. I love her so much. But why doesn't she love me the same way in return?"

Harrington's love for Paulette reflects a popular conception of love, but it is certainly not inner-liberating. Inner-liberated persons realize that they alone are in charge of their love feelings toward another but that they have no control whatsoever over what another person chooses to think and feel. If the object of their affections chooses to reciprocate, they accept that as a bonus, but they know they cannot always count on that happening. If they continue to offer their love to another regularly and it is not returned in any way, shape, or form, after a time, it is likely that they will turn their affections elsewhere, where they are more likely to be appreciated. "After all," these persons reason, "I'm lovable, I'm a decent, loving human being—and I want to be close. I certainly don't expect persons to love me just because I happened to love them at a particular point in time. But I hope somebody will. Let me look around."

A THOUGHT FOR YOUR FILES (CHOOSE ONE)

Defective Thought	Effective Thought
I can only really "love" someone if he loves me back.	I can love another, but I can't be responsible for what the other person thinks or feels in return.

Loving others comes easily to the inner-liberated person because he does not take the rejection of his loving overtures as personal. Therefore, he is not afraid to risk sharing with another the fact that he loves her, even if she does not respond in kind.

In the mid-sixties, during the week that I was awarded my doctoral degree from Columbia University after years of sometimes arduous work, I felt particularly loving about life and people. I asked one of my colleagues, Marvin Tulman, whether he thought it was "proper" for me to place a box of cigars and some candy in the school cafeteria with the inscription, "With my compliments to colleagues and staff." "Jerry," he said, "never wonder about etiquette when it comes to expressing something loving and nice. If the feeling is genuine and it is loving, always act on it." I did. His was an inner-liberating thought. I have found that you never really go wrong if you permit yourself spontaneous acts of giving, sharing, loving. The world can use all the loving acts it can get—proper etiquette notwithstanding.

I–THOU

Martin Buber, the existential philosopher, wrote of "I-Thou" relationships as being the most significant among mankind, and inner-liberated loving is composed of an I-Thou quality. ("I am a special human being. You (Thou) are a special human being too.")

I-Thou implies that you appreciate the humanness in another to the same extent that you appreciate humanness in yourself. I-It, is used when you treat another "objectively"—like an object. There are times when treating another as object is fashionable.

During war, our propaganda machines quickly establish that we are fighting "gooks," "reds," "nips," or other impersonal demons who are subhuman. When we accept this, we are enabled to be ruthless, thoughtless, and even to kill. Before killing a chicken, it is wise not to know its name or that it has children, not to have seen it grow from a small chick. No one likes to chop off the head of a fish that was a pet. But on a fishing expedition, the "objects" of the catch can be sliced down the middle and gutted with hardly a visceral stir.

A THOUGHT FOR YOUR FILES (CHOOSE ONE)

Defective Thought	Effective Thought
I know what this person is trying to say, so I'll pretend that I'm listening and then tell him what I think. I've heard this type before.	This is a person and he is unique. I'm going to listen to this person on his own terms. I'll probably learn something and at least get closer to this human being at this time.

Loving the "me" in you

If I am not feeling very good about myself as a human being but I am attempting to have an I-Thou relationship with you, that might be less than inner-liberating. Inner-liberating loving is predicated on the notion that "I love the 'me' in you." Accordingly, if there was not very much in my "me" that I loved, it would be quite impossible for me to find any parts of you that I loved. In order to love another person you must identify with parts of yourself that are in that person. If you do not have parts of yourself that you like, at least to some extent, how will it be possible to appreciate these aspects in another person? What we can identify with most often in others are their basic humanness, their weaknesses, their capacities for joy, for loving, for being lonely—if we ourselves have come to appreciate these as our own personal qualities too. If we have kept ourselves insulated from human experience, then naturally there would be little we could identify with in others— hence we could not be loving, at least in the inner-liberating sense. Loving the "me" in you requires that I have an appreciation of "me."

Empathy, not sympathy

Empathy means "feeling *with*" while sympathy means "feeling *for.*" Inner-liberated loving requires empathy, not sympathy. The empathy offered must be accurate empathy at that. Empathy means you place yourself in the shoes of another. Sympathy, on the other hand, suggests that you stay in your own shoes and peek out over the fence. "There but for the grace of God go I" reflects sympathy. Certainly sympathy for another human being is better than treating the other as subhuman. But sympathy can often be debilitating. In fact, there are many who properly resent sympathy. For example, an unemployed laborer might say, "I don't need someone to feel sorry for me, I need someone who will give me a job." But very few persons can be burdened with an excess of empathy.

Someone who accurately empathizes with the unemployed worker might not have a job to offer either. However, accurate appreciation of the worker's situation as a human being can be valued. Most everyone wants to be appreciated. It is certainly not very pleasing to feel misunderstood. The pleasures of feeling truly understood are so great, in fact, that people will go to extreme lengths to seek this experience. ("At least so-and-so understands me. That's more than you ever did.") The person who has learned to accurately empathize can offer the understanding that many people are hoping to find.

In order to be able to empathize accurately, the first step is to go out and attain many life experiences. Allow some loneliness, alienation, joy, rejection, exhilaration into your life. Only then are you in a position to accurately choose empathic thoughts as part of loving others. Only then will you be able to sense accurately in others their hurts or joys or other special feelings, to be able to come close in approximating that same feeling in yourself at the same time that this other person is sharing with you.

Kinds of listening

If I were to tell you the intense difficulty I experienced in breaking my smoking habit some years ago, how I found myself jittery and nervous, how I longed, with genuine heartache, for a smoke for months and months, even a year, you might listen in one of several ways: critically, laughingly, sympathetically, or empathically. The loving way would be empathically.

Listening critically. "I hear what he's saying about all that jittery nervousness and all that. He's had a tough time and probably still does, if he hasn't changed his attitude. He was weak."

Listening laughingly. "What a character. Boy is his situation funny. Cute what people like him go through in order to get over a dumb thing like smoking."

Listening sympathetically. "Oh, that poor unfortunate fellow. Too bad, too bad. Amazing what some persons go through."

Listening empathically. "I myself can feel some of that jitteriness that he is talking about. I can feel some of the tension in my own wrists, in my own stomach, as he is talking. I sense viscerally what it is that he is sharing. And as he is sharing, I can feel some of that ache that he experienced. Of course, what I am feeling is not exactly what he was experiencing, but I sense that what I am feeling comes pretty close."

Of these four kinds of listening, it is the empathic listening that is obviously of a loving nature. Inner-liberated persons do not listen empathically to everyone, nor could they listen that way all the time. Sometimes they, too, listen critically, laughingly, or sympathetically. After all, they are only human, and their purposes, as they come into contact with others, vary. There are times when some persons need to be listened to critically—when they are being interviewed and evaluated for a new job, for example. Inner-liberated persons know the different kinds of listening that they offer others, and choose the kind that best suits the moment and their purposes.

Caring

Caring is not something that one does automatically. It is an attitude that one chooses to have or not to have in a given circumstance. For example, if someone that you know begins to relate to you what a difficult time he had yesterday, you can, by an act of volition, decide whether you wish to pay attention, to *care* for what he is telling or not. It is a conscious decision that you can make. Once you decide to care, the process is self-perpetuating. The person sharing, sensing that he has someone who "gives a damn," generally tends to share more openly. As this person shares more freely, you can then decide to care even more, or if you have opened up "a can of worms" that you are not prepared to continue to deal with, tune that person out. If you tune him out, that too is an act of volition.

Unfortunately you cannot pay equal attention to everybody in this world. All you can offer your fellow human beings is a generalized nonpossessive warmth and a sense of respect. However, since there are several billion other humans on this planet, it stands to reason that your generalized warmth is going to be spread rather thin. Usually it's far better to care deeply about the people around you more than you care for those with whom you have no real contact.

Whenever two or more people tend to become close, there is a natural tendency among them to refer to themselves as "we." In your family, if there is cohesion, you must occasionally refer to yourselves as "we." (Italians, Jews, Blacks, Christians, Catholics, Arabs, or whatever group(s) you tend to identify with are your "we.") Even at work there is a "we" ("we in our department," "we in this building," "we fellow administrators," "we workers," etc.). Whenever there is a "we," unfortunately, but realistically, there is also a "they." It is generally true that "we" all tend to treat the "thems" somewhat less benignly than we treat one of "us."

A THOUGHT FOR YOUR FILES (CHOOSE ONE)

Defective Thought	**Effective Thought**
I was *infatuated.* I can only have one true love in my life.	I was in *love.* I can love numerous persons at various times, all at once, but to different degrees.

Steve loved the whole world. He sent out "vibes" to all the peoples of Asia, to everyone behind the Iron Curtain, to his fellow man everywhere. When he looked around the room at his colleagues, all he could feel was disdain. "These uncaring bastards," he thought, "all they care about is themselves when half the world is starving."

Steve had also abandoned his wife and kids because they didn't care enough about others. "And look at those wealthy people in the stores, walking through like robots. Unconscious. They sicken me."

Surely Steve was a very loving person—in the abstract. He seemed to do infinitely better when it came to caring about others the more they were geographically distant, more in the abstract. But when it came to really listening to and caring for those that were in his immediate environment, even members of his own family, he didn't seem able to muster the capacity to empathize. There are many people like Steve.

A middle-aged woman who said she had lived in and traveled to many parts of the world enrolled in a graduate course in group dynamics that I was teaching. After the first session, she called me aside and asked if she might do a written report instead of staying and interacting with the group of twelve other students, men and women who varied in age from twenty-one to fifty-five. "Why?" I asked.

"Because all of these people in the group are from Long Island." "That's true," I said. "But what's wrong with that?" "I can't take them," she said. "The people from Long Island are so spoiled, so empty, such nothings." Since the woman speaking was herself from Long Island, I asked, "What makes you so down on Long Islanders?"

"Well," she said. "I was with my husband in South America for more than two years, and there we got to know real people. They knew what life was about down there. The e people here, on Long Island, what do they know of li e? They're not real people. They haven't suffered. The / haven't lived." I didn't argue, but I thought differently.

People everywhere are struggling to make a life for themselves. All kinds of people, even Long Island people. So are Chicago people, California people, Mexicans, and the English. We are all persons struggling in our own way with the stuff life is made of. All human beings, to the best of my knowledge, experience elements of joy, despair, loss. All persons try, in the best way they know, to make a good life for themselves.

Pay attention to the person sitting across from you at the table. Hear deeply the human being who is sharing something with you in your own home, members of your immediate family. Really listen to some of your colleagues at work. Keep "in touch" with real, specific individuals who are in front of you every day. Inner-liberating love has a spiritual quality, and to find meaning and purpose by truly caring for another is a means of transcending yourself.

Cold as it may sound, inner-liberated persons rank other people according to a hierarchy so that they can avoid confusion when it comes to making certain necessary choices. They fully appreciate that they cannot be all things to all people.

It is a fact of life that all relationships are based on value given for value received. For example, your spouse or lover cannot be expected to remain true to you if you are not returning something in kind to her. If you were engaged in an affair, it is only reasonable to expect that were she to know about it, the character of your relationship would be subject to change. Interpersonal relationships are contractual in nature, although the contract is usually informal. As in all contracts, there is value given for value received.

Unfortunately we cannot have everything in this world. Sometimes we have to make choices, even among friends. It is reasonable to explain to one of your friends that your relationship with her, no matter how close, is subject to a pecking order (how objective that sounds) and that she may not be first on that list in a given instance. Most good friends can accept that. Of course, this list is fluid and changes with circumstances. However, it is wise to remind yourself periodically of your priorities in your relationships. There is no reason to mislead or confuse either your friends or yourself.

What does your hierarchy of relationships look like? Pause and make a list right now. Be fully cognizant that it is, and has been, subject to change from time to time, depending on conditions. Yet once you have developed your own list, you will have clarified for yourself those persons who are most important to you—and why.

A THOUGHT FOR YOUR FILES (CHOOSE ONE)

Defective Thought	Effective Thought
My relationships with all people are on an equal basis.	I have a hierachy of interpersonal relationships.

OPENNESS IN LOVING OTHERS

Openness was explored in the previous chapter, and it is this very same quality that is the third ingredient in inner-liberated loving. By being personally open, it is meant that you show on the outside very much of what is going on inside of you. That is, you are transparent and undisguised, there is a oneness between what you seem to be and what you really are. Of course no human being can be totally transparent all the time. Also, since we've agreed that there are parts of you that are entirely personal, it is impractical for you to be totally transparent.

The most significant moments in truly inner-liberated loving are those when you stand psychologically naked. In such a moment of mutual loving, two persons come as close together as is humanly possible: psychologically, spiritually, and physically fusing—a symbiotic merging of two entities. However, inner-liberated persons have learned that as close as they can sometimes get to another person, there are still certain elements of self which are independently personal. In intense moments of mutual love, the self is practically forgotten as the two separate entities momentarily blend into one. The key word here is "momentarily." In actuality, in love you continue to remain a separate individual—who gets close to another but does not remain "fused" on a permanent basis.

THE LOVABILITY CYCLE DEEPENS

Combining the trait of loving with that of being lovable enriches the lovability cycle, introduced earlier. Being both lovable and loving makes you an excellent candidate to be loved by others (no guarantee, of course).

Effective Capability

While loving others is often a powerful reason for wanting to live, it is our achievements, our accomplishments, that reflect what our life has been about. Working successfully toward exciting, challenging, achievable goals makes life worthwhile. Have you started to write that novel that you always intended to write? Are you building that house in the country as you planned long ago? Are you preparing for that marathon run you hope to complete? Have you started to diet toward that ideal figure yet? It is goals such as these that make our lives purposeful, worthwhile, and exciting, but only when we sense we are progressing toward them. The feeling that you are making progress toward these goals is as important as—perhaps more important than—the goals themselves. After all, life is essentially a process rather than an end. It's your achievements that give you this sense of progress.

If you clarify *one or more goals* for yourself—goals that are well worth working toward, that are beyond your immediate grasp—you will find that day-to-day existence becomes easier if you make some (even slight) progress toward this larger goal. Once you establish for yourself a worthwhile dream, a dream that takes some struggling and some energy, you will then have to find the way to carry yourself toward it. Dr. Viktor Frankl did just that when he was held in the Nazi concentration camps. During all the time he was imprisoned, he never for a moment forgot his ambition to write about the theory he was developing, and he worked on that theory even while imprisoned.

While he was a prisoner, he found the will to survive unbearable hardships so that *someday* he could write his book about logotherapy, his own brand of psychology, much of which derives from his experience and observations as a prisoner.

He decided that he would utilize the harsh experiences that he was faced with in the concentration camp as a basis for his theory. This plan made the unbearable bearable. His accomplishments continue to this very day, and his dream continues to be realized.

It is through your larger purposes that you can transcend any confusion or tension that occurs in your day-to-day existence. It is your sense of larger purpose that permits you to endure, even enjoy, situations that another person might find intolerable. It is this larger purpose that gives you a sense of order and direction, even when things, externally, might seem very disordered and out of synch to others.

Recently, a thirty-six-year-old graduate student in one of my classes, Floyd, shared with me the value of finding personal purpose for himself. Floyd decided that he was going to add a large extension on to his modest home. What was special about this project was that he had determined to do all of the construction work entirely on his own even though he didn't know the first thing about construction when he initially began. "I couldn't even put in a nail straight at first," he said, "but for some strange reason—I don't know exactly what got me started—the whole idea of building this room became an obsession with me. I think I might have gotten the idea from a magazine or somewhere—anyhow the whole idea just took hold of me. So I began reading up on building and construction. I bought a set of tools and made the plans, and off I went. My wife was amazed because she never saw me act this way before. I got plenty of expert advice. You'd be surprised how much advice and help they give you at the lumberyard if you ask. I found out that I can learn how to build almost anything once I start asking questions of the right people. People really like to help, if you ask in the right way.

"This was the first time in my life that I ever undertook something big like this. In fact, when I was a kid, I couldn't even read the plans for building a model airplane. Oh, it took me over five years to finally finish this room, but I loved every minute I worked on it. It was all done in my spare time. I couldn't wait to get home from work so I could get to it. Even Sundays and holidays. It was great. When it was completed, it was beautiful. One of the best things I've ever done in my life. You can't imagine the thrill, the satisfaction, I still get from that room. Everything in it was done by hand. I look around it and feel so proud.

"Sure I got discouraged every now and then, but if I didn't get what I was doing properly the first time—for instance, like one time the ceiling beams were put in all cockeyed at first—well, I just took them apart and started all over again until I got it just right. Imagine, every square inch of this beautiful room entirely on my own. I'm keeping my eye out for another project now. The way I've come to think is that I can do almost anything if I put my mind on it. I love to build now."

What is most significant about this is that Floyd, until that point, was not considered, either by himself or by those around him, "handy." He became handy because he clarified what he wanted to do. He simply chose the thoughts and asked the necessary questions so that he could become sufficiently competent to do what he passionately set out to do.

It's purpose first and skills second. Find your purpose— and then you will find the energy to master the necessary skills to achieve this purpose of yours. Through your worthwhile purpose you will find the stamina, energy, and enormous resiliency to keep going. What is it that makes a goal worth your while and qualifies as being inner-liberating as well?

INNER-LIBERATING GOALS

In order for a goal to qualify fully as inner-liberating, it must meet four criteria:

(1) It must be genuine and heartfelt (intrinsically worthwhile to the doer)

(2) It must not be based on a speed factor (no serious deadlines)

(3) It must be achievable but challenging

(4) It must not be subject to unmanageable outside interference by uncaring others

Let's examine each of these in greater detail.

Through the conquest of loneliness anxiety you can expect to come up with a purpose for your life that is yours and yours alone. It will be genuine and heartfelt. In my view, each of us is, in the broad sense, an artist. For some, their whole lives are a painting. In no case is it acceptable for you to accept a life that is meaningless and petty.

Decide for yourself what you really want to do that is very special. Are you a secret poet? A musician? Are you a student of human nature? Establish in your mind that you are somebody special. Don't take on something as a purpose just because someone foists it upon you. Review your wants and goals, those that you clarified earlier. What project, what talent, can you develop to help you move little by little toward those goals of yours?

As I said, one of my most exciting purposes, certainly the most heartfelt for me, is the working toward significance as a painter. I did not decide to be the best painter this world had ever seen, but rather to become the best painter that I could possibly become in my lifetime, according to my own standards. For the first time in my life, I was to be the judge of my own success—and no one else. I would not leave that final judgment to a gallery, a critic, not even to art teachers. I began a serious study of art, and after the expenditure of considerable time and energy as a student, plus a period of apprenticeship, I believe that I am well on my way to becoming what I intend to become. From this pursuit I have developed a sense of accomplishment that far transcends anything I had previously experienced. It's my goal, my choice—and it is quite personal. I proceed toward my goal at my own pace.

An inner-liberating project is not seriously predicated upon some external deadline. Deadlines, inner-liberated persons have learned, can do just that—help make you dead. When you have an externally imposed deadline, you are pressed to march to someone else's drummer, to meet someone else's needs, to be responsive to outside influences.

Deadlines, in a very practical sense, are of course necessary. Book-publishing schedules are built upon deadlines;
travel plans without a timetable can go for naught. But
inner-liberated persons never set serious deadlines for
themselves in terms of the projects that give them the highest level of meaning. They might meet externally imposed
deadlines, but only if the external schedule is in concert
with their inner schedule.

Speed most certainly kills, and I'm not referring only
to amphetamines. When you set yourself up to be in a
rush, you cannot expect to find your own tempo, and it
is working at your own tempo that makes it possible for
you to accomplish the most significantly. If my graduate
student, Floyd, had attempted to construct his room addition within a strict time deadline, he might have never
undertaken the project. Recall that he had to take apart
an entire ceiling so that he might do the job to his personal satisfaction. If he had been rushed by a deadline,
he would have missed out on the deep pleasures of a
quality job, well done, done to his own level of personal
satisfaction. And if your project is not personally satisfying, it has little to do with your achieving the necessary
purpose needed in life.

In fact, it is the general lack of qualitative work, the lack
of doing anything to one's personal satisfaction, that makes
so much of present existence so empty for so many.

School probably started you thinking along the lines of
speed. The "fast class," the "slow class." "All right, now
who's got the answer?" Look at all those bright kids who
get their hands up first. The teacher tells a parent, "She's
very quick. You should be proud of her." Yet all of the
greatest accomplishments that people have made were not
done in a race (unless they were in track events). The great
symphonies weren't written in a rush, nor were the great
inventions or paintings made in a day. They were accomplished by those who had a steady, unyielding commitment
to a goal, who plodded on ahead regardless of what others

thought, regardless of what others were doing with their time.

If you happened to be in a class where some of the students arrived at the answer sooner than you did, it would not be surprising if you began to view yourself as less than competent, at least in that subject area. There is too great a premium put on quickness in most schools.

A THOUGHT FOR YOUR FILES (CHOOSE ONE)

Defective Thought	Effective Thought
I'm not too bright when it comes to that.	I can understand practically anything. I'm in no great rush. I have my own style of learning. It might take me a little longer than the next fellow. However, I assure you that I can understand practically anything, given sufficient time—and of course, if I really want to.

Inner-liberated persons have learned that they have their own rate for learning. They have decided that they are going to enjoy being genuine, even if slow, learners. They have learned to take their own pulse, generally to look neither to the left or right to compare themselves to what the fellows next to them are doing when moving toward their purposes. Instead, they keep their eye on what it is that they have set out to accomplish, and then they go on and on, relentlessly, steadily, regularly moving along toward their target.

They can tell you in advance that their target, whatever it happens to be (as long as it is humanly achievable), is a "dead duck." They just pursue and pursue until they accomplish whatever it was that they have set out to do. It might take them a month to do what someone else might do in a day or a week, but that does not deter or disturb them in the slightest. (Remember the story "The Turtle and the Hare.")

An inner-liberating purpose is a purpose that is not too easily realized. If it is too easily achieved, there is too little excitement connected to it. If your chess opponent is weak and you win easily, the victory leaves you little to celebrate about. But if you were to tackle an opponent who was a bit more than your equal, there would be a challenge connected with enterprise.

DeKooning, the painter, has been reported as responding to the question "How do you know when you are finished with a painting?" with "I am never finished. In fact all the paintings I do, I see as only a *part* of the one single painting I am doing in my lifetime. Each painting is only part of this whole, which I never ever expect to fully finish."

This is an inner-liberating concept. Whatever project you undertake—even when it appears finished—might serve your inner-liberating purposes better if you choose to see this so-called completed project as only a portion of a larger project, a whole lifetime project that you are committed to. So if you write a "finished" essay, consider it only a part of your total body of work. Or if you successfully grow flowers one season, see that success as only part of your lifetime gardening mission. Similarly with any of your purposes or dreams.

Be sure to get hold of a project that has substance to it, that is challenging and long lasting. Bite off just a little more than you can chew. Then go at it bite by bite. It's not the large size of your project or dream that keeps you from realizing it. It's getting started. Setting small and "chewable" goals is much easier. Remember: "Life is hard, yard by yard. Inch by inch, it's a cinch."

A THOUGHT FOR YOUR FILES (CHOOSE ONE)

Defective Thought

Things didn't work out and I'm crushed. I've failed. I'm a failure.

Effective Thought

Things didn't work out this time, but what can I take from this experience to help me succeed if I choose to try again? The project might have failed, but I didn't. After all, I'm not the project.

When I started writing this book, I knew from the very start that nothing or no one (other than myself) could possibly keep me from completing it. All I needed was a pen and the paper.

In order to write any book—or letter, poem, or essay—or to build, or to accomplish anything, all that is needed is sufficient resolve. You do not need any special talent to write or build to your own level of eventual satisfaction. No matter how bad your early drafts look, you can go over and over and over them again—until what you have done finally meets the reasonable personal standards that you establish *for yourself.*

In my view, I can write a reasonably articulate phrase or two. So why not a sentence? Then why not a paragraph? And if I can write a reasonably articulate paragraph, of course why not a chapter? And why not a dozen or more chapters? In fact, how about a whole book? Why not? There is nothing in the world that keeps me (or you) from doing this if there is really sufficient resolve to do so.

Absolutely no one told me to start writing this book (or some of the others I've written). I started all by myself, with a germ of an idea, a desire, something I deeply felt was worth saying—and with a pen and paper. Then I worked. Writing. Mostly rewriting, over and over again, until what I wrote met my needs—my own purposes. And then after

a while, I took it to the public, in the form of a publisher
—and here it is. I had full control of all the writing until I
decided to take it to the public. Until that point, this project
was fully under my own control—and might have stayed
that way if I had wanted it to. It was not entirely inner-
liberating to expose myself to external deadlines, an editor's critique, and so on. But at that point the project was
well under way and had already met my deeper, *personal*
purposes.

A THOUGHT FOR YOUR FILES (CHOOSE ONE)

Defective Thought	Effective Thought
I didn't really write that. I got so much wonderful help.	I did that. Others offered advice and some excellent suggestions. But in the final analysis, it was my creation— on my own. If it wasn't for me, it would never have been.

Once you decide to ask others' opinions and seek their
approval for your work, be it a painting, a musical composi-
tion, or your garden vegetables, it becomes an entirely
different ball game.

You must learn to *never* take the opinions of others as
seriously as you take your own. Certainly you will have
to deal realistically with others' views and various outside factors once you go to the marketplace with your
personal project. It is therefore important that you not
go public with your project until you have satisfied yourself first.

Many jobs and projects are subject to unmanageable outside influences. If one of your purposes was to be elected
mayor, that would not be inner-liberating at all. It might be
a worthy goal and you might very well achieve it, but it
would not be an inner-liberating goal because too many
other people and factors outside of your control—such as

your "image," community politics, and the response of those "over" and "under" you—are involved.

A THOUGHT FOR YOUR FILES (CHOOSE ONE)

Defective Thought	Effective Thought
I have no special talents.	I am creative and talented on my own terms.

I once had a barber tell me that for his five-dollar fee he could give his customers a fifty-dollar haircut, a five-dollar haircut, or a fifty-cent haircut, but that most customers hardly knew the difference. If he liked someone, he gave them a fifty-dollar haircut. If not, the fifty-cent job. "Only I know the difference," he said. His inner-liberating purpose might become "giving high-quality haircuts," simply for the sake of the quality of the experience.

The most valuable purposes in terms of inner liberation are those that are yours and yours alone. If you establish that you want to become the best painter that *you* can possibly become—not comparing yourself to anyone but your old self—then it is an inner-liberating purpose.

To play the guitar better than you ever did before, to cook a gourmet meal better than you ever had previously, to offer more exciting and sensual love to your partner than you ever have before—all these are potentially inner-liberating goals, goals that can add greater meaning to your life. Just be sure your goals meet all four criteria, and you're on your way.

THE CAPABILITY CYCLE

As you tend to feel capable, you tend to achieve. Achieving naturally reinforces the feeling of capability.

Now you have set in motion cycles of lovability and of openness—for moving toward a deeper calm—and cycles of loving others and of capability—for finding more significant purposes. Therefore, calm and purpose will conspire to offer you a sound basis for greater adventure, which is Centering-Step Six.

Chapter
· 7 ·
STEP SIX:
Enjoying Adventure

Adding adventure to the dimensions of calm and purpose will complete the centering process. Adventure requires risk taking. You have to take some chances; you can't play everything safe. But at the same time, you must keep intact both your sense of inner calm and your sense of purpose. This takes knowhow.

Two personality traits are vital. These two traits are particularly effective in that they can be achieved by your thoughts alone: they are not contingent upon any other person's reaction, they are reality-based, and they enhance your sense of inner calm and personal purpose. The traits are spontaneity and sensuality.

Effective Spontaneity

Spontaneity is subject to serious misunderstanding and subsequent abuse. Such abuse can result in unnecessary hardship, as with Carla in the example that follows.

Carla was overworked and deserved a chance to "let go," to be irresponsible for a change. But the office party was not the ideal place for her to enjoy this release, at least not in the way that she went about it. When the music began, Carla did a dance combined with a series of gestures that made Mata Hari look tame. To top it off, she went over to her boss and let him have a piece of her mind. She unloaded everything that had been pent up and bothering her at work over the past year. It just was not the right time or place for these spontaneous actions. Carla was spontaneous all right, but effective, no.

In just one hour of spontaneity she had managed to jeopardize her relationships with her boss and her colleagues and and her chances for advancement. Net point: don't let your spontaneous acts louse up aspects of your life that are of lasting importance to you.

Zorba the Greek, in Kazantzakis's novel, also did a memorable dance. It was eminently more effective than Carla's. The huge log-tow rig that he invented and worked so mightily and so long to build came tumbling down in a crash. It was a tragic failure. But instead of crying in frustration and despair, Zorba looked up to the sky and as if there was music coming from the heavens, he spontaneously created a marvelously beautiful and crazy dance with his partner. The dance was absolutely spontaneous, and it integrated perfectly with Zorba's philosophy of extracting the maximum satisfaction out of life regardless of what hardships life might next dish up. His dance personifies the spirit of inner-liberated spontaneity.

A THOUGHT FOR YOUR FILES (CHOOSE ONE)

Defective Thought	Effective Thought
I like to play it safe. Trustworthy friends, famous brands, no side roads, only major highways. I like to know well in advance what to expect. I'm not one for surprises.	I enjoy getting off the beaten path. I learn and discover when I take risks. I enjoy adventure and excitement. I enjoy risks in relationships, loving, leaving, sex, sensuality, money, telling what I feel, failing, and changing, but all in concert with a sense of inner calm and personal purpose.

"Letting go," "suspending critical judgement," "acting with abandon," "letting your hair down"—all of these are forms of spontaneity. Although it is true that during actions that are truly spontaneous there is an absence of critical thought, a thought-choosing process is still going on. You still remain *responsible* for the thoughts you choose when you are relaxed or intoxicated; but even though you are actually responsible, you take a rest from feeling responsible. You rely on your preprogrammed intuition, instinct, habits, rather than critical thought. It is not only pleasurable but also necessary to rest your critical faculties once in a while. However, you can only do this comfortably when your instincts and habits have been trained through practice to serve your best interests (Zorba) and not your worst (Carla).

At the times when you decide you can trust your instincts and let yourself operate intuitively, you become free. Free to have fun, to experience joy and happiness. You can function casually—with grace, ease, and with a sense of humor.

A THOUGHT FOR YOUR FILES (CHOOSE ONE)

Defective Thought

I'm tired of playing it straight, Damn it. I'm letting go—no matter what.

Effective Thought

I'm letting go. This is a good time and place to let go.

It is not very wise or very healthy to always be on guard, especially when it is unnecessary. I pointed out earlier that while inner-liberated persons are expert in choosing effective thoughts, they don't spend all of their waking moments deliberately trying to do this. Most of the time they rely on their preprogrammed subconscious mind to do effective thought selection for them automatically. Only when they find that they are in an uncomfortable situation do they take it upon themselves to consciously and systematically choose effective thoughts that lead them from inner *dis*satisfaction to inner satisfaction.

A THOUGHT FOR YOUR FILES (CHOOSE ONE)

Defective Thought

I'd better always be on the alert and keep trying to consciously choose my thoughts.

Effective Thought

I'm in a safe place. Good time to let go and stop being so critical and analytical. I'll just relax and trust my intuition. No need here to consciously choose effective thoughts, moment by moment.

TIMING

Timing is everything. Ask any baseball player. Ask your stockbroker—he'll tell you that the secret of getting rich is buying low and selling high. Carla's dance at another time might have been delightful and appropriate.

The onle real time is the present, "now." This very moment, while you are reading these very words, "now" is all you really have. All of your past present moments are already gone, and all that is left of them is your memory of them—which is quite distorted. As far as your future present moments go, none are guaranteed. You don't know *for sure* about the next twenty minutes, let alone tomorrow or years from now. That's why "now" is all you really have.

I am not suggesting, however, that you attempt to accomplish everything you ever wanted in this particular instant. What I am suggesting is that you learn convincingly how to handle your "nows" effectively. If you know how to handle "nows," your future looks great.

As for your past, the same holds true. If you handled your "nows" effectively in the past, then you've undoubtedly got a track record you can be proud of. History might never lie, but historians sometime do. Because our egos are so delicate, nature has protected us by providing us with a selective memory as a defense. Selective retention permits us to remember from the past only those aspects that serve our present ego needs. That is why the winners of a football game recall the plays quite differently than the losers do. That's why a teacher might recall a student's behavior in class that the student doesn't remember at all. The past is ashes. Nostalgia might help you get through a period of stress in your life since the choosing of thoughts about the past might bring on a warm glow, but the past is gone forever.

Enjoying here and now

If you handle "nows" effectively, your future stands to look good. Here's the best way to make "now" an excellent point in your life: in any "now," simply choose effective thoughts, thoughts that will make you feel sound and help you function at your optimal level. It's exactly what we've been exploring all along. If you're faced with a tense business meeting, choose the thoughts that will prepare you for it. "Better do my homework" might be the appropriate one. Having trouble sleeping? Choose thoughts that put you to sleep. Perhaps it's fleecy clouds or resting at the beach that proves effective for you. Upset because your friend is late for your appointment? Choose thoughts that permit you to enjoy the sunlight, the air you're breathing, or whatever proves effective for you rather than be upset over your friend's tardiness.

"Here" is where you always are

Every "now" occurs in a particular situation. Whether the "here" situation is comfortable or uncomfortable is essentially a state of mind. On one cold, blustery day recently, I spoke to an elderly man who was pumping gas at the local station. "Freezing cold. Must be tough working outside on a day like today," I said. "Not really," he said. "I like cold weather. I really enjoy it. It's my favorite." That's clearly a very effective attitude for him to have considering his job. Who is to argue with him about the pleasures of freezing weather? How you feel here and now is a matter of attitude. All you need do is choose the effective thoughts that make your situation satisfying.

The "right" place for spontaneity is always "here." Since you know how to make any given "here" quite satisfactory, all you need do is let go, providing of course that letting go is compatible with your inner calm and your deeper purposes.

SELF-TRUST

Professor Hopkins pulled his yellowed notes from his files. They were labeled "Lecture Twenty-one: The Romantic Period." Professor Hopkins had been reading this very same set of notes to his weary undergraduate classes for the last ten years.

Carol acted excited. She even made breathless sounds. But she thought to herself, "Why can't I let go? Am I doomed for life to keep faking to Frank that I'm having an orgasm?"

Richard tried vainly to smile. But his stomach was tight as a drum. Why is it that he couldn't relax even in good company? His stomach was always tense. He almost had to rehearse everything in advance before he let it come out of his mouth.

The main reason these persons were so nonspontaneous was because for one reason or another they had not learned to trust their intuitive inner selves.

Your inner self needs an element of surprise and spontaneity incorporated into it. My own self-picture, "Gentle-Flowing Brook," makes provision for spontaneity in that the brook ebbs and flows around various nooks and crannies in the woods, trickling and fumbling into various surprising turns. That's one reason I value this particular self-picture so much.

In addition to an improved inner self-picture, Hopkins, Carol, and Richard would all benefit from using auto-suggestion. For example, Professor Hopkins might reprogram his intuition with the thought, "When I get up in front of class without notes, some of the best ideas about the Romantic Period will arrive in the foreground of my conscious mind." Once his mind is reprogrammed, what he anticipates is likely to happen. Not only will Professor Hopkins benefit, so will his classes.

Carol's husband would benefit similarly if Carol learned how to reprogram her subconscious in the same way. If

Carol were to prepare herself to enjoy the "now"—experiencing all the pleasures that the "now" of being in bed with her husband has to offer—she would probably be able to have genuine orgasms. And if her husband wasn't doing all he could to help her have a genuine experience, she might even learn how to be spontaneous enough to risk telling him what it is that is really going on inside of her body.

Richard, the shy one, can also be helped. He too can reprogram his intuition to carry him along in social situations, perhaps by suggesting to himself that he will no longer be overly concerned about what others are thinking about him and his actions.

Risking

When I was invited to teach graduate school for the first time I was very pleased, and naturally I was quite anxious to do well. So in anticipation of each lecture, I prepared and prepared, even going so far as to haul a big box of books from class to class. These books (with certain places carefully marked in each of them), along with my extensive notes, were my security blanket. I had a great fear that I wouldn't have anything worthwhile to offer the graduate students if I relied primarily on my own ideas and instincts. At the conclusion of the courses, I asked the students to anonymously give my teaching an evaluation. I was astonished at how many wrote something to this effect:

"Dr. Kushel, the course was fine, but the reading from your notes and the books that you had marked up was quite boring after a while. I wish that you would have shared more of yourself and your actual experiences as a counselor and therapist. The few times that you did tell us about your real-life professional experiences were the best parts of the course.

P. S. Don't be afraid to be yourself. You seem to have a lot to offer."

Since that time I have risked being my spontaneous self many times, both in teaching and in my personal life. And through this process of risking I have discovered many exciting aspects of myself that would have undoubtedly remained unknown and untested if I had not become sufficiently self-trusting.

Just "being"

Many of us are afraid to just "be." We don't think enough of ourselves. And so we try too hard to compensate, to put on a show, to win the right to just "be." Obviously, this tendency stems directly from the concept that we discussed in the preceding chapter—lovability. Many of us do not feel sufficiently lovable to risk just being *ourselves."*

When a person remains on guard, even when there is very little or nothing to guard against, he succeeds not only in keeping others away but also in keeping himself from finding out what he can do. Inner-liberated persons, however, are not afraid to just be because they have come to appreciate the fact that they have nothing to fear from the outside world. They have learned how to choose thoughts that can carry them comfortably through almost any situation.

You are not a prisoner of circumstances

If you permit yourself to be more spontaneous, you might not be all that dependable for others unless they get to really know you. It probably wouldn't be a bad idea to get one of your T-shirts emblazoned with the warning, DON'T TAKE ME FOR GRANTED. Those who love you (that is, really listen to and care for you on your own terms) will not be confused because they will know "where you're coming from." The people who don't really listen to and care for you all that much might sometimes think you are unreliable.

In my own case, I may seem unreliable to those who don't really know me. After all, I know no thought is unthinkable. Who knows—if it makes sense to me, I might just take off cross country. I do not allow myself to be a mere prisoner of any situation. I might even decide to walk out in the middle of a meeting and be alone for a while. The freedom that such thinking affords me is critical to my inner liberation. Since I am confident that I can handle any "now," any consequences of my actions, I feel loose and spontaneous. And fundamentally I am more myself and therefore *more* reliable and stable.

A THOUGHT FOR YOUR FILES (CHOOSE ONE)

Defective Thought	Effective Thought
You can always count on me, no matter what. I'm "good old reliable."	Please never, under any circumstances, take me for granted. Unless you really know me, you might be surprised by my next act.

LETTING UP

That one should do better when he comes to care less is an interesting result of inner-liberated living. When a person stops pressing, stops trying too hard, he does better. Physiologists have noted that during athletic contests many athletes perform at maximum capacity when they are not overly tense, when they are not straining. In a game such as tennis, for example, hitting the ball with too much tension can actually throw off your timing. There are certain muscles that are used to thrust and other muscles that are used to restrain thrusting. When you are trying too hard, both sets of muscles go into operation at once. So in a direct sense you are thrusting and restraining your thrusting at the very same time. This obviously results in neutral-

izing your hard effort. It is much more effective to have only
a slight amount of tension, just enough to help you concentrate on the match. In that way, you will be sufficiently free
and loose to play your best game.

The same principle holds true in sports, sex, vocation, or
avocation. Pressing too hard, fighting to meet some intimidating external standard over which you have no control, can lead to ineptness or even a total paralysis and
blocking.

Not a prisoner of reputation

Your past reputation, good or bad, can be a terrible trap.
Even your own excellent reputation can become a noose
around your neck. Think your way out of this noose right
now.

Farrell, an extremely tense forty-three-year-old archi-
tect, came to me three years ago. Because he had established a marvelous reputation for being highly reliable
and competent, he had become trapped. Many people
(colleagues and clients alike) looked to him for advice,
and he was flattered. "One thing about me," he said,
"people know I'm good at what I do." It was only after
Farrell came to realize that the pressure of keeping an
excellent reputation was taking its toll on his insides, on
his nerves, that he began to choose more effective
thoughts. "I'm not my reputation," he later came to say
to himself. "My reputation is only an image. People will
have to learn to accept me for being me—and the me that
I am is far from perfect." When Farrell *decided* for himself
that he would settle for a lesser reputation, the strain
upon his nervous system eased considerably. Interestingly, when he let up on himself, his work somehow improved, even though he wasn't trying nearly as hard.

In a similar vein, Audrey, a highly accomplished artist, a
thirty-seven-year-old abstract painter, came for counseling
in the midst of what she described as "a terrible block."

Over the years, she had established the reputation for being, as one critic said, "a highly imaginative, vigorous innovator." Now, although her next show was only a few months away, she had become paralyzed with tension. "I don't think I can do it again," she said, fearing that she could no longer live up to the high standards she set for herself. Like Farrell in the preceding case, Audrey came to realize that her reputation was not her. Critics and others have their own perceptions, and she in no way could take responsibility for how others chose to think or feel. "My reputation is an illusion over which I have no genuine control." Once she ceased worrying about what others might think, she was able to go on with her work. Eventually she moved past this block, working at her own rate, and concentrated on painting for herself—"and not for what others might think." Audrey's reputation as an artist has continued to grow, even though she cares much less about what others think.

Later she told me, "At the time I was painting for critics, sometimes I wouldn't even please them. So no one was pleased, not even I. Now I paint to please myself, and so now at least *one* person is pleased even if no one else is." This is very effective way of looking at an activity. At least please *yourself.*

Permission to be imperfect

You do not have to seek perfection either in yourself or in others. Proceed at your own pace, spontaneously, and don't wait until you've perfected what you intend to do, whether it is approaching an authority figure, taking a trip, or even telling a joke. If you wait for the perfect time to do anything, that time may never come. Act first and then analyze your action. Willie Mays, the former center fielder for the Giants, when asked how he went about making a spectacular catch of a fly ball, responded, "I first catch 'em.

I leave it to you to analyze 'em." If you're waiting until everything is "just right" before you begin writing that book or taking that trip or approaching that interesting person, stop waiting. Act. Remember, regardless of what happens, you'll be able to handle it. If you fail, you will bounce back and move on toward becoming more effectively spontaneous the next time.

Some people have established impossible standards of absolute perfection by which they unfairly measure themselves and others. This not only leads to self-paralysis but also keeps them from enjoying the freedom to experiment —even the freedom to fail. Instead, the perfectionist doesn't even try.

There are people who are terrified to try to dance. "The only way that I would dance is if I had the proper training. Someday I'm going to take the lessons and really do it right." So in the meantime they sit around and watch others "make fools of themselves." But it is these so-called fools who are having a good time. Those who sit on the sidelines waiting for perfection to strike can often spend an entire lifetime watching the world go by. Accepting the fact that you might not be doing something to perfection, but that you are doing the best that you know how at that particular point in your life, is a very freeing and effective thought.

June, a twenty-five-year-old secretary, came for counseling because she was deeply afraid of meeting new people, especially men. Mainly, it seemed, she was intimidated by small talk. "What should I say to a man if there doesn't seem to be anything special to talk about?" she asked. "I just panic when there isn't anything in particular to talk about and I'm facing a person."

I discovered that she had had a very troubled history with the males. Her father was an alcoholic and generally unavailable when she was growing up. In addition, a clergyman she trusted seduced her when she was a teen-ager. For good reasons, she had very little confidence in her capacity to relate effectively with men. However, after months of counseling, she realized that much of her fear centered around being spontaneous. With small talk, there is no focus, no direction, and therefore if one tries too hard, as June usually did, it is only natural that one freezes up. If she were eventually to develop a healthy relationship, she would have to risk spontaneous small talk.

Once, June came to her counseling session in great panic. Her girlfriend had arranged for her to be invited to a mixed-singles party. "I really want very much to go, but I'm terrified. What will I say if I'm paired up with someone —especially if it's a man?"

"June," I said, "I want you to go out and be very *boring.*"

"Boring?" she repeated with surprise.

"Yes, I want you to go to that party and whenever you sit next to a man, I want you to make a special point of being very boring. Either say nothing or very little. If you must say something, make it a point that what you say is dull, uninteresting, even foolish."

She looked at me incredulously at first, but then she said slowly, "Okay, Dr. Kushel, if that's what you want me to do, I'll try." And she did. Fortunately, she didn't follow my instructions to the letter. Somehow she ended up being "interesting" to a very eligible young man at the party. Later on, June told me that every once in a while when she found herself facing someone and experiencing panic, she would hear my voice saying over and over to her, "June be boring. It's perfectly all right to be boring." Eventually June learned that she could be silent, even "boring," and still relate. The lesson has proved to be a lasting and useful one for her. (As a matter of fact, she married that young man.)

We limit our capacity to risk, to be spontaneous, to experiment, if we press too hard. Fear of failure, fear of not meeting some ideal standard of perfection, too often keeps many people from realizing their potential. Is there any way of knowing how many wonderful books have never been written, songs sung, dances danced, entire lives lived, because people were afraid to fail and so instead did nothing.

Resiliency

The ability to bounce back after you've goofed is a crucial element in living. You are bound to make human mistakes. Bouncing back confidently from these errors is essential. While Carla made a fool of herself by dancing erotically at the office party, even though she may have lost points on the job, her life still goes on. She can learn from her mistake. Certainly Carla, even though she risked imperfectly, is more alive than Professor Hopkins, who never chanced speaking to his students without his rusty, outdated notes. To risk spontaneously and louse up is still better than never to have risked at all.

A THOUGHT FOR YOUR FILES (choose one)

Defective Thought	Effective Thought
I screwed up. I'm just no good. I should never have eaten that whole cake. I'll never be able to get back on my diet.	I screwed up, but at least I really enjoyed myself, letting go of my diet for once. Wow, a whole cake. But, that's okay, I'm back 100 percent on my diet as of this very moment. Feels good to be on course.

BE SPONTANEOUS NOW

By accepting the fact that nothing can really happen to you that you will not be able to handle, you become free to let go. You pick your spot and and then cut loose.

Risk doing something that is not all that comfortable for you. Go over to the phone, perhaps right now, and call an old friend and tell him in all sincerity how much you miss him (if you do). Or go into the next room and tell your spouse something that you've been meaning to say for a long time. "Let it all hang out." If you are going to have sex tonight, really let go. Try something kind and new with your partner. Take a risk. Life itself is one big risk. If you want more "life" in your life, "now" is the time to begin.

THE SPONTANEITY CYCLE

Each time you succeed in being effectively spontaneous, you will be rewarded by greater joy, excitement, and adventure in your life. As spontaneous behavior is reinforced, you will tend to become effectively spontaneous again and again. You will have set in motion a cycle of being effectively spontaneous.

Effective Senses

Equally as important as spontaneity in achieving adventure in your life is to be "effectively sensual"—that is, to employ your senses in a focused, enjoyable, and qualitative way. The key to focusing your senses is of course the choosing of effective thoughts. We have a total of five senses: hearing, tasting, smelling, touching, and seeing. Focusing your thoughts in such a way as to have a high level of qualitative sensual experience is what inner-liberating sensuality is all about.

Your body is the house in which your feelings reside, and your thoughts are the key to the door. Your mind and body in reality are one. Holistic medicine, the most recent emphasis in health care, treats mind and body as a single unit. So before we begin to explore the effective thoughts necessary for you to achieve a focused, qualitative sensuality, let's look at the house that stores these senses and examine some of the basics for keeping it in good repair.

DIET AND EXERCISE

You get only one body per lifetime—one set of lungs, one circulatory system, one liver, etc. You had better take good care of your body. It is important to remind yourself that it is not like a car that can be traded in when it gets beat up and worn out. To abuse our body is to weaken considerably our opportunity for realizing maximum sensuality.

To keep your body in good health takes not only effective thoughts, but also effective action—proper food and exercise. Without an adequate diet and sufficient exercise, the housing of all your sensory equipment weakens, damaging your sense organs themselves.

If you are like most people, you have not found it all that easy to control your diet. Dieting does not necessarily mean losing weight, but rather controlling the food you eat so that you remain or become healthy. A good diet is really a lifestyle. For many, dieting means taking off unnecessary fat. For a few, it means gaining weight. I am not about to recommend a specific diet to you, but I can offer you a way to stick to whatever diet you eventually select. Any decent diet should not be just a crash weight-loss event but rather a steady way of life. Finding an optimal style of eating to fit your needs is important. Although it is only human that you deviate from your diet from time to time, you can by and large stick to it by choosing the necessary thoughts. You may sometimes have to resort to autosuggestion if mere thought choice on a conscious level proves inadequate. Through autosuggestion, you can program your subconscious with the necessary thoughts to counter the temptations that keep you from the diet you have chosen. Remember, it is you and you alone who put each mouthful of food in your mouth. No one can make you put anything into your stomach that you don't want in there. All you need to do is establish what the effective thoughts are that encourage you to eat the way you really want to, and then you simply reinforce these thoughts by acting on them.

Reggie, one of my clients, who was thirty-five pounds overweight, was having great difficulty staying on a diet that he had chosen for himself. He was helped by putting himself into a self-suggested trance. When in the trance, he gave his subconscious the following effective thoughts: "Reggie, you don't freak out over chocolate anymore. When you see chocolate, you just look away from it. It leaves you cold. You can easily pass it by." With this thought firmly implanted in his subconscious he was able to forgo chocolate cake (his nemesis), and each time he did so, he reinforced this behavior until bypassing chocolate became habitual.

Exercise requires action. You must translate your thoughts into behavior or there will be no exercise. Many persons resist physical activity. As with diet, I have no special regimen of exercise to recommend to you. Millions of Americans have taken to jogging, others to walking or tennis. This is commendable, but generally you should not permit outside pressures to supersede your own instincts about what is sufficient exercise for your own body. Unless it is your hobby or a particular purpose of yours to break athletic records, permit your own body to be your guide as to how much exercise is enough for you. Begin slowly. Add a little more the next time out. Exercise regularly, habitually—but don't overdo it. Listen to your own drummer rather than to that of the gang, the crowd, or the competition. Generally, noncompetitive exercise is more lasting and more healthful as the years go by than that which is overly strenuous and competitive. If you enjoy friendly competition in tennis, softball, or other sports, then by all means enjoy it. But never take the competition so seriously that you impair your health. After all, you have only one body to give to your inner-liberated lifetime.

SELECTIVE SENSING

It is your sense organs that permit you to experience life, that bring the outside world in to you. Yet everything that is brought in through your sense organs is filtered through your thoughts. Without thought, the light brought in by your eyes has no place to register. Without thought, the odor brought to you through your nose has no effect whatsoever. And so it is with all of your senses. Therefore, if you choose an effective thought to complement the lights, smells, tastes, sounds, sensations, you make it possible to mediate these inputs in such a way as to add to your control over the quality of your inner existence. Your task is to focus on the most effective qualitative inner experience, an experience that serves your best interest.

Take the problem of pain. Jon was attempting to repair the electric toaster. He was standing in the kitchen in his stockinged feet when the screwdriver fell off the ledge of the counter upon which he was working and landed squarely on his big toe. At the same time, he was concentrating on twisting two broken wires together—trying to repair the toaster. Which would be more effective—to continue trying to concentrate on twisting the wires, or to concentrate on the pain that was potentially in his big toe? In a microsecond, Jon, an inner-liberated type, acknowledged that his big toe had been hit and realized immediately that the pain would lessen after a few moments or so, so he stubbornly refused to pay very much attention to the event, continuing to apply his concentration and thoughts to repairing the wires. A little later he hollered "Ouch" and turned his attention to his poor toe. He held it and rubbed it. Since it throbbed only a little now, it was no problem giving it plenty of attention and concentration.

Let's analyze Jon's strategy. It made no sense to pay attention to (choose thoughts), to concentrate on the pain in his toe at first, because such attention at the moment of contact only heightens the pain rather than lessens it. Since in an instant Jon knew that nothing practical could be done (he could only wait for the pain to subside), it only made great sense to go on with his chore—repairing the toaster. *After* the pain had subsided, he acknowledged it.

Many times football players, or others actively involved in the heat of competition, fail to notice their injuries. Athletes have gone on to complete contests with broken hands, jaws, even noses, without even knowing that they had such an injury until after the contest was over. Such is the power of effective thought.

You choose thoughts to accompany everything that your senses bring in to you. Naturally, it is intelligent to scan all this material for a general impression, and then it is wise to concentrate only upon that which is worthy. This applies equally to sights, sounds, smells, flavors, or feelings.

If you go to a fish market, choose thoughts that keep the smells you don't care for from spoiling the time you spend there. If you have to look at certain persons at a meeting, make it your business to choose thoughts that permit you to see something worthwhile—perhaps the way shadows fall on different faces, the nuance of color on clothing, or whatever it is that makes the time spent more palatable for you. If you must listen to hard-rock music you don't like while chauffeuring some teen-agers, choose thoughts that either permit you to tune out the music entirely or find some aspect of the music that you can enjoy. Perhaps even permit yourself to enjoy the beat. Choose thoughts in similar fashion about everything in your environment that your senses bring in. It is totally within your capacity to choose thoughts that permit you to "tune in" and "tune out" whatever you want.

Tune out unpleasant sensations. Tune in the pleasant. For example, one of the highest pleasures, sex, can be enhanced. Heightened sexual experience requires the selection of effective thoughts. Orgasm is more a product of the mind than it is a purely physical act. The sensitivity, warmth, and feelings of mutuality that are part of optimal sexual intercourse are all brought about by thought choice. Deepening the sexual experience between partners can take place by choosing such thoughts as:

"This is a loving experience I am having."

"I enjoy what I am experiencing. This brings me great pleasure."

"I am not afraid of a new position; I love risking in bed."

"I see, touch, taste, smell, and love you."

"I care about what she/he is feeling now."

THE SENSUALITY CYCLE

When you learn to be more effectively sensual, you begin another cycle—the sensuality cycle. It works like this: as you begin to sense more effectively, you enjoy more; since you enjoy more, you permit yourself to continue to experience more effectively. And so the cycle goes on.

You have now learned how to start in motion a number of cycles within the dimensions of calm, purpose, and adventure. Each of these cycles is self-reinforcing and furthermore, each tends to reinforce the others. In a larger sense, the three *essential* inner-liberating dimensions—calm, purpose, and adventure—reinforce each other synergistically.

You have now completed the six steps necessary for you to attain a high level of personal inner liberation. Let's inventory all that you have accomplished.

Chapter

· 8 ·

The Synergy of Inner Liberation

O nce you have learned the effective attitudes that provide for calm, purpose, and adventure, you will automatically reap the benefits of a synergy in which each element strengthens and deepens the others.

Calm, when achieved in combination with a sense of purpose, tends to be deepened and enriched; the reciprocal is true for purpose. More specifically, when you choose thoughts that permit you to feel more lovable than before, you tend to become calmer. Having attained an improved sense of calm, you are in a better position to clarify your purposes, and being purposeful tends to make you even calmer. The same holds true for calm and adventure, and purpose and adventure. All three qualities are compatible and operate synergistically. The synergy of calm, purpose, and adventure, in short, the synergy of inner liberation can be diagrammed as on page 165:

You will notice that there are discrete areas to each of these dimensions and also areas of overlap. In the very

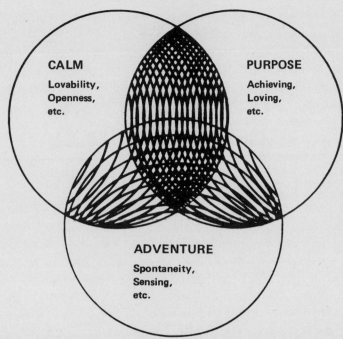

center, calm, purpose, and adventure all overlap. These are the areas when the greatest synergistic action takes place.

For example, consider the theoretical situation of Paul, who has learned, through choosing effective thoughts about his lovability and openness, to become calm. As he became calmer, he clarified for himself that one of his personal purposes was "to write significant poetry." The writing of significant poetry (significant according to his own standards, of course) added an even deeper sense of inner calm. Now, feeling both calmer and more purposeful, he was in a better position to take worthwhile risks to become more sensual and spontaneous, more adventurous, than before. All three dimensions took added power from each other, and Paul was the beneficiary of this natural synergy. Inner-liberation is the fruit of this synergy. Greater, clearer purposes emerge. A deeper, more pervasive sense of confidence, of inner calm, develops. There is an exciting, increasingly adventurous interaction with life.

When I first came to understand this synergy, I thought it was a "high" that was probably too good to last. But much to my surprise and pleasure, I have found that it does not diminish with time at all. The truth is, it gets stronger and stronger. It is self-reinforcing.

A Starter File of Effective Thoughts

Now that you are thoroughly familiar with the centering process, you will find it relatively easy to create all sorts of thoughts that are personally effective for you—thoughts to help you through virtually any situation in which you might find yourself. Some thoughts will be derived solely from either your calm, purpose, or adventure; others will be created by combining them.

Below is a starter file of effective thoughts. You may wish to add to this file some thoughts of your own that you have discovered to be personally effective. Then when it becomes time for you to choose an effective thought to help you with a particular situation, you can refer to this thought file as a starting point. If you don't find exactly what you need here, create for yourself the thought that is needed. But when you are through with a particular effective thought for the moment, don't discard it. File it here for future reference, as a periodic reminder of what works for you.

EFFECTIVE THOUGHTS
(A Starter File)

ALONENESS

You can sometimes get very close to other persons, but in actuality there will always be a part of you that is totally alone. When you were born, the mold was broken and thrown away. There was never another person exactly like you on the face of this earth, and there never will be again. You were born alone, and you will die alone. Others can get very close to you and you can get very close to others, but there will always be a part of you that no person but yourself can fully experience. The important thing to remember is that you not *run* from loneliness, but allow yourself to experience it. You need not be lonely if you come to terms with your aloneness.

APPROVAL

You cannot ever be responsible for what another person thinks about you. Other persons are responsible for their own thoughts—just as you are for yours. Although you can enjoy having others approve of you, you can never rely on them to do so. If you act primarily for the sake of approval of others, you might very well end up pleasing no one. But if you act in a way that you yourself approve of, then at least one person will be pleased. And of course that one person is you.

BODY

Your body, as well as your mind, has intelligence. It speaks to you—if you listen to it. It will tell you when it is enjoying something and when it is not. It has many other important messages for you. Learning from the "neck down" is as worthwhile as learning from the "neck up."

CENTERING

You cannot do everything. You have to edit your existence, day by day. You have a center—if you allow yourself to experience it. Around your center, you can integrate everything. You can discover what you are about, your own tastes, your own values. You can appreciate life qualitatively if not quantitatively; for you can only do one thing well at a given time.

DEATH

You are definitely going to die in a relatively short time. Even if you live a century, since it is estimated that the world as we know it will last for about fourteen billion years, your lifetime is only "a drop in the bucket." You will be in proverbial eternity for a long, long time. There will be no exception made in your case, no matter how well connected you are or become.

EXPERIENCE

No one other than you can experience your life. You can attempt to live vicariously through others by watching TV, dreaming, reading novels, seeing movies, or the like. However, it is quite possible for you to do many things firsthand in your own lifetime if you so choose and if you take appropriate risks.

FACTS

You cannot change absolute facts. However, sometimes something appears to be a fact but really isn't. All you can do about a fact is face it. However, if something is not a fact but an opinion, then you have a perfect right (and the capacity) to choose your own opinion. You can learn how to choose effective opinions—that is, opinions that work for you instead of against you. "Correct" opinions (thoughts) are not necessarily effective opinions (thoughts).

FEELINGS

You own a marvelous sensory apparatus. You can experience a tremendous amount in your lifetime, even in a moment or two, by fully employing the capacities of your senses. You can learn how to see more effectively, hear more clearly, smell more keenly, move more gracefully, and feel more sensitively. You can enrich your moment-by-moment existence at literally no cost.

GUILT

It makes no sense whatsoever to feel personally guilty over that which has already been done. What is done is definitely done. There is no going back. It makes sense to learn from your errors so as not to repeat them. But nothing worthwhile is accomplished by self-blame over that which cannot be rectified. You cannot possibly go back in time.

HELP

You can ask for help whenever you want it, or need it, without being weak. Maybe you appear to be independent but you are really just afraid to ask for help —even though you may really need it. Embarrassment, fear of rejection, and social taboos often keep you locked into loneliness. Remember: it's perfectly all right for someone to say no to your request for help.

HOLISM

You are all of one piece. Your mind and body are one. Although, in a basic sense, your thoughts, feelings, and behavior are all of one piece also, it is useful to remember that your thoughts are the "key," your feelings are "where you really live," and it is your behavior that "goes public."

HUMANNESS

Whatever you are, you are all that you have. At best, you are only human and subject to all the mistakes and foibles of human kind. You are by no means perfect.

ILLNESS

If you get ill, it will be your own illness. It will be your pain, and you will have to deal with it. You do have some powerful resources in your mind and body that you can employ, if you so choose, to help you deal effectively with such circumstances. Your thoughts, especially, can be a powerful ally. It is your body and mind that will have to overcome the disease. Take care of them.

JUSTICE

There is no such thing as absolute justice. It is an abstract concept and you cannot always expect to get "a fair shake." Sometimes you will get more than you may think you deserve, and sometimes less. Evil is not necessarily punished, and good is not necessarily rewarded. Do not expect to be justly rewarded for your good works. Do what you do because you want to, not because of the justice you hope to receive.

LOVABILITY

You can be lovable, but there is no guarantee that any other person, aside from yourself, will fully appreciate you for what you really are. Lovable means able to be loved. Most, if not all children are born cuddly, small, and able to be loved. But even so, some are not loved. The fact that they are not loved does not mean they are not lovable. No one, lovable or not, can make another person love him. Chances are, however, that a person who feels lovable will eventually become loved. But no guarantee.

LOVING

Loving involves listening to and caring for others on their own terms without trying to superimpose your values on them. Loving involves an I–Thou attitude, empathy rather than sympathy, and personal openness. You cannot own the own the object of your love. Loving others adds clear purpose to your life.

NOW

This present moment is all that you can ever be certain about. It is yours to experience, to enjoy. It will soon be gone. You have only a limited number of present moments allocated to you. However, you can choose to use each of them as you see fit. The past is gone forever. Your selective-recall processes will distort your memory to protect your ego. The future is not assured in any way.

PURPOSE

It is much more productive to spend time searching for purpose and meaning than searching for happiness. Happiness is a by-product, not an end in itself; if you search for it, it tends to vanish. Purpose and meaning, however, are worthy ends, especially if your purpose is a passionate one. If a person has a "why" for existence, then the "how" becomes secondary, yet really discovered. Purposes usually involve loving others and achieving successfully according to inner-liberating standards.

REJECTION

You cannot possibly be rejected by those who do not really care about you or know you. If a person does not really care about you, he can't really listen effectively to you. If he cannot really listen to you, then it follows that he can't really get to know you, at least for what you really are. And if he does not know you for what you really are, then it is not you that he is actually rejecting but rather his illusion of you. Therefore, it is difficult to take much so-called rejection seriously.

RELATIONSHIPS

All interpersonal relationships are really quite conditional—value given for value received. This becomes clearer in long-term relationships. Even your closest friend or your spouse accepts you on a conditional basis only. If, for example, you decide to "cheat" on this friend, the character of the relationship is bound to change. There is a hierarchy in one's relationships; you value some more than others.

RESPONSIBILITY

You are fully responsible for yourself and your actions. Actually, you are responsible for yourself and your actions whether you are able to acknowledge it or not. No one else is ever responsible for what you think or feel. You are, in a real sense, in charge of your own destiny, whether you want to be or not.

RISKING

You can make life exciting and adventurous by intelligent risk taking. Effective risk-taking behavior can be learned and applied. You should take risks often—to avoid lethargy and dullness.

ROLES

In everyday life you are often required to play various roles. There is a significant distinction between playing a role and doing a job. Playing the *role* of manager, for example, can be quite different than the actual act of managing. Playing roles is often necessary, but role-playing by definition is never really a very serious business. Doing a job is almost always serious business. One can often do both well, but it is important to be aware of the considerable differences between the two. Never confuse the roles you play with your real inner self.

UNIQUENESS

There is a unique rhythm inside you. It is a rhythm all your own that you can dance to or march to as you wish. No one else can hear it. You are not crazy just because others don't hear this music. They have their own, if they will listen for it.

WORRY

There is absolutely no value in worrying. You can turn your problems into projects, and then you will not have worries. You might have due concern, but not worry. "Worry" implies spinning your wheels unnecessarily. "Concern" suggests taking proper steps, one at a time. Worry is a complete waste of time—in every way. It serves no valid function whatsoever.

You may wish to include here some of the Effective Thoughts from the Thoughts for Your Files that have appeared throughout this book. But more important are the effective thoughts that you develop on your own. This starter file is just that—a beginning. It is up to you to create (or borrow) whatever effective thoughts you need for the optimal inner liberation.

Thoughts such as those in the starter file can be linked together and grouped in patterns, creating what I call "inner-liberating lines of thought." Whenever you find yourself in a situation that is less than satisfying, less than what you have targeted your life to be, all you have to do is to figure out an inner-liberating line of thought—a line of thought that works for you to make your inner life more satisfying. These lines of thought are bound to lead you into a plan of action which helps your outer life too. It makes no sense whatsoever to permit yourself to choose indiscriminately thoughts that make you nervous, ineffective, or anything else that is less than optimal.

For example, suppose that you have been married for a long time but, through a strange combination of events, you have also "fallen in love" with another woman. You are having obsessive thoughts about this other woman, guilt-producing thoughts that keep you from sleeping soundly, from performing your job efficiently, from relating as warmly as you would like to your wife and children. What are you to do? More specifically, what inner-liberating lines of thought should you choose that will do you the most good?

At this junction it behooves you to make some decisions about the direction your life is taking. The decisions can be made intelligently when you consider what the principles of calm, purpose, and adventure indicate to you. Imagine that your newly developed inner-liberated self is speaking to your old self about calm, purpose, and adventure, and see how each of these relates to your obsession with this other woman:

Calm. It is important that I retain a sound level of inner calm in my life. To think about this other person overstimulates me. Is this what I want? Do I want to feel overstimulated? No. Okay, so I shouldn't choose thoughts about her. If I can't do this at a conscious level, then I'll have to use autosuggestion techniques.

Purpose. What does this other woman have to do with the purposes of my life that I have established for myself? Does thinking about her or getting further involved with her add in any way to my achieving my purposes? What are my life's purposes again, anyhow? My main purpose, of course, is to have a satisfying inner existence. Does being involved with her add to that? (If yes, then continue to be involved. If no, then don't get involved any further.)

Adventure. Being involved with this other woman is certainly exciting and adventurous. But what about calm and purpose? Are those dimensions being realized sufficiently as well? (If not, then it is apparently no time for you to let go, or experiment. If yes, then by all means cut loose and permit yourself the excitement of this involvement with this person.)

By weighing the calm, purpose and adventure factors in any situation you are able to arrive at a balanced decision.

Through the perspectives of calm, purpose, and adventure, you provide yourself with a centering point that can lead to focused action rather than caprice.

In many situations, it is a good idea first to devise an inner-liberating line of thought and then to impress that line of thought on yourself by speaking it out loud.

Practice carrying out an inner-liberating conversation with yourself. Have the pre-inner-liberation "you" get in dialogue with the inner-liberated "you"—the "you" that you were meant to be, the "you" you are becoming.

Practice giving yourself effective inner-liberating *advice*, sound, effective thoughts to choose in each of the following situations:

- Your boss calls you on the carpet for not doing all you can on the job.
- Your spouse tells you that you are not participating sufficiently in the responsibilities of running the household.
- You find that, for the moment, you are very worried about where your next dollar is going to come from.
- A waiter has given you very poor service. The entrée was served without the vegetables, and everything took too long to serve.
- Your child has just failed a subject in school that you know full well he has the ability to pass with ease.
- The dog has urinated on the new sofa.
- Your neighbor tells you with authority that your spouse has been cheating on you.
- Your new car was dented in the parking lot, and the offender is nowhere in sight.

How did you make out? It takes some practice and imagination to put inner-liberated theory into operation—but once you've learned how, it becomes habitual.

In the next chapters you will learn even more about how the inner-liberating principles we have explored can be applied in real life. In these chapters we will focus upon "effective emotions," "genuine intimacy," and specific issues in "risking." You will be shown the value of referring back to your file of effective thoughts so that you might deal more easily with issues that face you in day-to-day living.

Chapter
· 9 ·
Effective Emotions:
Expression and
Control

To what degree, under what circumstances, and toward what ends do you permit your emotions free reign? How do you moderate your emotional expression so that it serves you best? What are the effective inner-liberating thoughts that produce a more satisfying emotional life for you?

Emotions are feelings—visceral experiences, internal *responses*—that result from the thoughts you choose. If you take away the thought, you also take away the *feeling* that the thought produces. An infant is born with a simple sense of pleasure and pain. There is little that is as pure as an infant's total expression of glee and joy. Nor is there anything more intense than that infant's scowl and cry of displeasure. Gradually, as the infant's capacity to think is refined, his emotional responses become proportionately more complex until he has acquired a full range of emotional expressions. These are all *learned* by choosing thoughts. The child learns fear, joy, worry, anger, love, confidence, hate, and many more emotions, some producing inner satisfaction, others disrupting the quality of his inner life. He learns that loud sounds are not necessarily always to be feared. Take a small child to her first football game at a crowded stadium on a Saturday afternoon. At kickoff the crowd lets out a mighty roar. The long-awaited game is finally under way. But look at the child. She is crouched in stark fear—the roar of the crowd (most naturally) is frightening her half to death. So she looks dependently to you for guidance.

"It's all right," you say to her. "It's all right. No need to be frightened," you say as you pull her close to you. "This is just a game—and the crowd always yells at the kickoff." And so she learns from you that there is sometimes pleasure in "yelling," and she adds still another lesson to her emotional vocabulary.

Here is some of the emotional vocabulary that most of us have learned to use:

Anger	Happiness
Anxiety	Hate
Calm	Innocence
Confidence	Jealousy
Depression	Joy
Despair	Liking
Disgust	Love
Ecstasy	Mellowness
Fear	Sadness
Generosity	Tension
Guilt	Worry

There are many feelings that escape accurate description. Words at best approximate feelings. Yet it is with words that we create the thoughts that bring these feelings to life. The key that controls your feelings is firmly within your grasp. You know how to choose effective thoughts, thoughts that lead to a more satisfying emotional existence. "More satisfying" includes the full range of human emotion, so your key permits you to let yourself go emotionally, to be stupid and foolish, even to be excessively emotional should circumstances warrant such feelings. Occasional emotional excesses can serve as useful stimulants. However, "paralyzing fear," "ulcer-producing anger," "bile-producing jealousy," or "heart-attack-producing worry" are defective. It is through your choosing more effective thoughts that such emotions can be readily brought under control.

CONTROL IS NOT REPRESSION

To regularly repress an emotion can lead to psychosomatic illness. A person who walks around with a smile on his face while he is burning up with repressed fury risks psychosomatic heart disease, peptic ulcers, migraine headaches, backaches, and even more severe diseases. Inner-liberated control of your emotions is quite different from repression. If you hardly ever get angry, it may look to others as though you are holding back your true feelings. But if these others knew how you really were looking at life, they would see that you are not repressing angry feelings but that in fact you are not experiencing these feelings at all. You, for example, might call me a dirty name, but if I did not presume that you were really referring to me, you would hardly expect me to be angry. This, in essence, is how inner-liberated persons insulate themselves from feeling anything at all that is unwanted or useless.

Fear

Whenever the inner-liberated person experiences one of the less than satisfying emotions—anger, worry, guilt, jealousy, etc.—he quickly asks himself, "What am I *afraid* of?" After he identifies what it is that he fears, and removes the basis for that fear, he finds that the secondary emotion—

anger, jealousy, etc.—simply dissolves. It is not repressed or held back—it simply vanishes; the fear upon which it has been based has been removed. Of course, if an effective line of thought cannot be found to overcome the fear, then the secondary emotion will continue to gain momentum, and another tactic will be needed. However, since inner-liberated persons have so many effective thoughts in their repertoire that help them overcome most fears, it is not usually necessary for them to go beyond this first strategy.

Once you have perfected your "I can handle it" attitude and have acquired all the traits that go with calm, purpose, and adventure, you will rarely feel intimidated, put upon, or threatened. When you have worked-through and accepted the various inner-liberating facts (such as "life can sometimes be very unfair," or "part of you is truly alone"), you will rarely be caught short and in turn frightened. Of course, the few times that you are caught short, you must immediately begin a working-through process to accept certain facts so that you can overcome the fear you are experiencing. More specifically, when you get angry, as you inevitably will from time to time (being caught short), you must not deny or repress this feeling but instead, quickly and energetically change your mindset and examine the basis of the fear that has produced this unwanted emotion.

There are in this world obviously some conditions genuinely worth fearing—pain, actual danger to yourself, actual danger to your loved ones, etc. The animal response to fear —characterized by an increase of adrenaline in your system, a tight stomach, a clenched jaw and fist, and shortness of breath—is a natural response, the "flight or fight" response, so necessary in nature. With the increase of adrenaline, we are able to muster a surprising amount of energy to deal with actual emergencies. Men have been known to leap over seven-foot walls when frightened sufficiently, whereas normally they could just about make it up a stairway. Women have been known to fight off assailants literally twice their size when sufficiently excited by fear. Fear can be an extremely useful and valuable emotional response. But unnecessary fear can do us tremendous harm. Those who operate in a *fearful* emotional state unnecessarily and too often produce flight or fight physiological stresses—adrenaline, the tensing of the stomach—but in a repressed form. Consequently, they harm both their bodies and their emotional systems. In addition, they often act out and harm those around them.

OVERCOMING UNWANTED ANGER

Fear is the basis of anger. If a fear is warranted, the anger that results is warranted too. If a bear emerges from the woods and frightens you, you run. You end up angry that the bear intruded in your path and sent you sailing. Quite reasonable. If your friend doesn't meet you at the appointed hour and you wait and wait, your *fear* that you will be left, or that you don't count to your friend as much as you thought, leads to frustration and anger. Is your anger warranted in this situation in view of what you have learned about inner-liberated living? Of course not.

If you did not have the unwarranted fear, then no anger would have resulted. The way to counter anger in this case is to simply remove the unwarranted fear. Choose thoughts such as this: "I don't know how important I am to this friend of mine. I know that I may be of some importance to her, but she also has her own hierarchy of relationships and needs. In any case, I am still a lovable person. So why be fearful and then angry? I'll just make it my business to enjoy myself while I am waiting. Perhaps I'll sit down on the curb and take a sunbath and wait to see if she turns up. If not, I'll go on to lunch by myself and enjoy my senses. Such is life."

Fear is merely a state of mind. In the same way that unwarranted fear can lead to unnecessary anger, it can also lead to other unwanted, usually useless, emotions—worry, guilt, and jealousy.

Feigned anger can be useful

If you decide that the anger you are experiencing is useless (as it generally is), you can easily feign anger rather than really experience it, thus saving your adrenaline, your stomach, and your heart.

One of my clients, Joyce, a twenty-seven-year-old nurse, was experiencing debilitating anger toward her son. However, she learned to control her young son, Jason, by feigning anger, giving him a stern look. Sometimes she clenched her fist and even stomped her foot. But inside, Joyce learned not to be angry at all. She simply came to realize that her son responded to the impression that "Mom is really angry." Her imitation of being angry got him moving much more quickly than her former windy explanations and uncontrolled anger did. By pretending anger, Joyce produced exactly the same effect as she would have had if she had actually torn up her insides with real anger. Since Joyce had developed a batch of effective thoughts to prevent being manipulated by others, and since she was secure regardless of how Jason behaved, she had overcome the basis for genuine anger toward Jason.

Overcoming worry

Worry is a word you could readily eliminate from your vocabulary if you didn't need it to describe what so many *others* do. Inner-liberated persons make it their business not to worry about anything. They do, however, replace worry with *due concern* when appropriate. Certainly it is wise to make plans for future contingencies. This is due concern. "Due concern" implies creative anxiety and a plan of action, whereas "worry" suggests the useless spinning of your wheels—busily going nowhere.

It is possible to worry about everything that has fear as its basis. You can worry about retirement, your job, your relationships, your health, your loved ones, the political situation, money, your life, your death—or even fear itself. But worry accomplishes absolutely nothing.

Worry is based upon the fear that something unpleasant or negative is going to happen in the future. Then, through our imagination, we viscerally experience this negative event. We think of our loved ones out in a car on the highway. We hear the screeching brakes, the crash; we see their bruised and bleeding bodies. We shudder. Our palms sweat. Our adrenaline pumps. We anguish—physically as well as mentally. It is real as far as our bodies are concerned, and the toll on our hearts, our stomachs—our lives —is real.

Yet most of what we worry about never takes place.

Recently I flew to California to give a lecture. When I arrived, the airline reported that my baggage was lost. "We think it might have gone on to Hong Kong," the clerk said apologetically. I decided in advance that I was not going to worry, even though a portion of a book manuscript (quite irreplaceable) was in my suitcase. Here was my line of reasoning:

"First of all, I will not worry because it will not change anything. If the bag and the manuscript are lost, I'll take care of that step by step. All I really have in this life are my mind and body anyhow. As far as the clothing in the bag —well, that is all replaceable. It will cost some money, but I can take care of that. As far as the manuscript—well, that will hurt. So—ouch. If it is gone, I'll just start on another. Who said life is fair?

"After all, here I am in a wonderful place and since I have a permanent sabbatical attitude, I'm going to enjoy myself —even if I wear these same clothes every day that I'm here, or even if I have to go out and buy some. But then again it is also possible that my baggage will show up, and if it does, I'll be in good shape."

Needless to say, the next day the bags were found and sent to my hotel with apologies. Honestly, I lost no sleep, had not one bit of anguish (other than momentarily, until

I reminded myself of the proper mindset and chose the necessary effective thoughts). Worry is just not part of my inner-liberating bargain with myself.

One of my clients shared a similar attitude that he had developed concerning his twenty-year-old daughter, who was driving around late at night. "Then I figured out that as much as I didn't like it, there wasn't anything that I could do about it. She's old enough now to take responsibility for herself. God forbid, if she got into an accident, all I could do is pay for her hospital bills, come and see her, show her that I care, and try to help. But worrying wasn't helping at all, so I decided to stop it; and I did."

We usually don't worry about something at the moment it is happening because when it is actually happening, we must deal with it instantly. You're not in the *process* of worrying while the boss is telling you off—you are too busy taking care of the situation then and there. If you stick yourself with a pin, you aren't worrying that you will be stuck with a pin—you are too actively engaged in saying "Ouch" and moving the pin away so that you won't be stuck again. When dealing with the "here and now," there is no time to worry. Think to yourself: "What if the worst happens?" See yourself dealing effectively with it, and then forget about it.

The next time you find yourself thinking ahead about some dreadful thing that might happen, take your imagination one important step further. Imagine that the worst has actually happened and figure out how you will survive. Imagine that the plane you were planning to take crashes. See yourself as badly injured. You crawl around for help. You are so very busy surviving or trying to survive that you have no time for worry. You will be able to ask yourself the three calming questions: What time is it? "Now." Where am I? "Here." Who is that person I am with? "Me." No matter what your situation, providing your mind still works, you will still be able to choose effective thoughts. You know that you will handle it—even should the worst take place—

once you have developed an inner-liberating attitude.

Next think of this—the dangers of an air crash are less than if you were to drive your car. Due concern, not worry, will prove helpful. Take an airline with a good safety record, and improve the odds in your favor. Listen to the flight steward as you are given instructions on exits and emergency procedures. Due concern again. Go and enjoy yourself. Certainly if worry were to help, it would be worthwhile for you to choose worrisome thoughts. Since worry offers absolutely nothing except ulcerating prospects, face the facts of life, treat the worrisome thoughts with due concern—and forget to worry ever again.

OVERCOMING USELESS GUILT

If worry is based upon fear of what's ahead, guilt is fear about what has already happened. And if worry is useless, then guilt—genuine, unrelenting guilt—is even more useless.

It makes sense to make amends for something you are sorry you did, and it is intelligent to make plans not to repeat your errors. But again, it makes no sense to worry—especially about what has already happened.

If yesterday or sometime in the past you said or did something that was unkind to someone—it serves no purpose whatsoever for you to feel guilty. You cannot undo that which you have already done. You had better spend your time doing something positive for that person now, if still possible, rather than lament what you should have done.

Some will argue that if you have committed a crime you ought to feel guilty and punish yourself. But it does no good to "get even" with yourself. If a government finds you guilty for a wrongdoing and penalizes you with prison or a fine, that makes some sense—if such punishment acts as a deterrent for subsequent wrongdoings. But it makes no sense whatsoever for you to penalize yourself. For example, if you are found guilty for speeding, you can accept society's punishment, especially if the punishment suits the offense. But there is no need to punish yourself twice. Your response to any "wrong" act that you've taken, should be present and future oriented, not past oriented. "What can I do now or in the future that can help me avoid undertaking such a wrongdoing again?" is a sensible question. But self-beratement or self-punishment (prolonged guilt) does nothing for anyone, least of all you.

Once I unfairly scolded my daughter when she was about five years old. I apologized, "Lynne, I'm sorry." My daughter, much wiser than I, retorted, "Sorry's not enough." And she was right.

Once a present moment passes, it will never be yours to spend again. At least not in reality. You might dream or fantasize about what you might have done or what might have been, but in reality there is no going back and doing it over. Life is not a movie. Therefore, to worry about what has already happened (feeling guilty) is perfectly useless. It keeps you from using your present moments much more productively. "Sorry isn't enough!"

We all make mistakes, do foolish and even stupid things. After all, we are only human. Since it makes no sense to berate ourselves, what should we do?

Take a tennis game as an example. Your doubles partner makes a strong shot. Your opponent returns softly. You move in for the kill. But for a moment you take your eyes off the ball, and you miss what should have been an easy point for your side. "Sorry," you say to your partner. He gives you a disappointed look. "Damn it," you say to yourself, "I'm an ass. I should have kept my eye on the ball. I really let him down. I know that I can do better, too. Oh, do I feel rotten. I am a bum."

Examine what you are doing. "I am a bum." This is a self-fulfilling prophecy. Is this self-deprecation doing either you or your partner any genuine good? Of course not.

New game point. Opponents are serving. You miss it

again. (Why not? You've already called yourself a bum.)

How might you have better handled your mistake on the tennis court? Retake. Take II. (Remember, as only in books and movies, not in real life.)

The ball is returned softly to you after your tennis partner hits a resounding smash to your opponents' court. Once again you mis-hit. This time your inner-liberating line of reasoning leaves you guilt-free—and with a self-fulfilling prophecy that is much more positive and just as realistic.

"Oh, I mis-hit. Damn it. Goofed. Okay, that's over. Let me visualize that stroke again and imagine that I hit it properly, without taking my eye off the ball. Okay, memory, store that more productive picture for next time." You are ready now to get on with the next play. "You're a good player, still."

OVERCOMING USELESS JEALOUSY

Jealousy can be one of the most insidious and debilitating of all emotions. Like with worry and guilt, the underlying emotion at the root of jealousy is also unnecessary fear. Eliminate the basic fear and the jealous feelings will dissolve. The usual fear behind jealousy is the fear that you won't get all that's coming to you in this life of yours.

When you think that someone is getting more than you, having it better than you, taking something away from you, you can become jealous. You may not feel jealous if your neighbor drives a new Oldsmobile if you happen to drive a new Cadillac. But you might get jealous if suddenly he is able to afford a Mercedes. "Where does he get the money? He must be doing all right." You fear that you won't be able to do "all right" too. You might try not to feel jealous, but deep down it's often there. "I'm not jealous. I'm glad for him," you say to your spouse. But even as you speak these very words, there is a dryness in your mouth betraying the lie in your words.

Years ago, one of my close friends, Irving, "beat me out" on an important academic post. At first I denied to myself that his good fortune bothered me. "The best man for *that* job won, that's all. I'm glad for him," I said to myself wryly.

What made matters worse was that shortly after he won this job, someone arranged a gathering in his behalf. I was invited. "Great, Irv," I said, "I'm really proud of you," squelching my honest pangs of jealousy.

Finally, after I could stand it no longer, I walked up to him at his party and called him aside for a few moments. I looked him in the eye and said, "Before we go on, I've got a confession to make." He waited. "Irv," I said, "I just want you to know that although I'm glad for you as a person, I'm also very jealous of you, because I wanted that job."

My confession cleared the air. I could then deal honestly with him for the first time. Then later I could authentically say "I'm genuinely pleased for you" and mean it.

By acknowledging my jealousy, I was able to begin to deal with it and also face the fears that underlay this wasteful but normal emotion. By admitting I was jealous, I was able to develop a line of effective thoughts that put the jealousy to rest. The line of thought went something like this:

"First of all, Irv is Irv, and I am me. I'm glad to be me. I've got my life, my style, and they suit me. Sure I'd like the job he's got at this point of my life, but in actuality I'm not doing too badly myself. I'm certain that some other people wish they could be doing as well as I am. Wherever you go, no matter how far up or down, there's inevitably someone doing a little better than you and someone doing a little worse. What's more, I'm still lovable. I've learned to have a great life regardless of any situation. So, Irving, I honestly wish you well."

Most of us experience human pangs of jealousy from time to time. "Why should they (the football players, the movie stars, the Rockefellers) make all that money for what they do? Look at how hard I work, and I don't get nearly what they do!" "Why is it that he got recognition for that when what I did was just as good, perhaps even better?" "I could have written better than that myself."

Jealousy results from the fears that arise when we compare ourselves to others. If we didn't compare ourselves, we wouldn't be fearful and jealous, especially if we didn't compare ourselves to those who seem to be doing better than we are. Yet such comparisons are quite normal. It might help for a moment or two to compare yourself to someone who is worse off than you, but the satisfaction from this approach generally doesn't last long.

A little bit of jealousy can sometimes be useful. It could give you the impetus to get started on that project you've long had in mind ("If he can do it, I can do it too"). On the other hand, jealousy that paralyzes, that poisons, that makes you miserable, makes you do things that deep down you'd rather not be doing, can readily be eliminated or at least seriously reduced by taking the proper inner-liberating line of thought. Here are the steps:

Acknowledge right off that you are jealous. When you keep denying, even to yourself that you are envious or jealous of another's good fortune, you keep yourself from dealing with it. If you speak directly to the person you are jealous of and say, "You know I'm really jealous of your good fortune," you can then have a much more honest relationship with that person—if such a relationship happens to be important to you.

Ask yourself: What am I afraid of that is making me jealous? Is it that you are not feeling sufficiently lovable or attractive? Is there a fear that you will never gain sufficient recognition in your own right? Is there a fear that you can't have a good life for yourself? Do you fear life and opportunities are passing you by?

All fears such as these can readily be overcome by inner-liberated thinking. Lovability and attractiveness are part of inner calm. It's pretty hard to stay jealous of anyone when you remember that you have mastered the techniques of calm, purpose, and adventure.

All your emotions, including guilt, worry, even depression, might be worth experiencing to a certain extent, but as one of my clients said recently about feeling depressed, "It's an okay place to visit, but I'll be damned if I want to live there."

ENJOYING

Most of this chapter focused on getting rid of or controlling unwanted emotions. Having done that, you are left with the pleasant ones—at least most of the time. Joyful experiences, ecstasy, fun, are all part of the spontaneity that was discussed earlier. In fact, this entire book and the line of effective thoughts presented here are designed to bring you your fair share of the pleasant emotions—calm, purpose, and adventure—so that you can enjoy being centered.

Sometimes, of course, it becomes necessary to moderate or curb joyous emotions too, and the control process is exactly the same. You simply ask yourself what it is that is making you so confident, then choose those thoughts that will make you feel less confident and smug. Thoughts such as the following will readily bring you down to earth when necessary:

"I'm only human."

"I, too, will meet the great leveler in due time."

"I can easily be replaced, in many ways."

"As well as I seem to be doing, there is someone doing better than me. As the pitcher Satchel Paige said, 'Somethin' might be gaining on ya.' "

"I put on my pants in the morning one leg at a time, just like everybody else."

Chapter
· 10 ·
Genuine Intimacy:
Autonomy

C lose, intimate relationships with spouse, family, friends, and some colleagues are important. Still, there is a part of you that no matter how close you become to another is reserved for you alone. It is the part of you that is totally special and unique, that makes you a separate and very important individual. Although you might value affiliation, closeness, and commitment even more than the next person, if you consider yourself inner liberated, you still remain independent.

Becoming close to another is not difficult once you have mastered the art of deep listening to and caring for another on that person's own terms. Earlier we explored how to listen empathically, keeping an I-Thou attitude with another, and how being genuine yourself creates closeness to another. You enter the other person's world, listening, seeing, experiencing, as if you were that person yourself. When this happens to you in return, there is a mutual love.

SELF-RELIANCE

Inner-liberated persons tend to be autonomous, independent people. They are self-reliant and fully appreciate that
they are fundamentally alone in this world. How, then, can
they be such "loners" and still maintain warm, intimate,
nurturant relationships with other human beings? How do
they artfully accomplish living in a loving fashion with other
persons without offending those who might want to
smother their need for independence?

The question for inner-liberated persons is not how to be
intimate; since they are loving persons, intimacy often
comes easily to them. The question for them is, "How can
I be more effectively intimate?"

Effective Intimacy

Desmond Morris, in his book *Intimacy*, describes twelve
steps in increasing the level and intensity of intimacy, from
the most superficial to the deepest. Step one is eye-to-body
contact. Step two is eye-to-eye contact. And so on, until
finally contact is genital to genital. Probably the deepest
level of intimacy, not described by Morris, is soul to soul.
Certainly individuals can get very close to each other both
psychologically and physically. You can be intimate with
colleagues at the office, with your spouse, your children,
your parents; yet each of these requires different kinds and
levels of intimacy.

There are four levels of intimacy:

LEVEL I: "I can share very little of what I really think and
feel without censoring."

LEVEL II: "I can share *some* of what I really think and feel
without censoring."

LEVEL III: "I can share a *great deal* of what I really think
and feel without censoring."

LEVEL IV: "I can share *everything* that I really think and feel without censoring."

Inner-liberated persons consider a Level-III intimacy with the persons they are closest to as the most effective. Level-IV intimacy is a fused state where two persons are fully blended into one, and although it is possible for some, it is not considered a rational objective. Instead they prefer to be very intimate (Level III), but at the same time they reserve space for some privacy and space of their own.

Before you can be truly intimate with someone else, you must first be intimate with yourself. That is, you must acknowledge everything that you think and feel to yourself. You must not shrink from taking account of your own thoughts, even your most frightening ones. Everything you choose to think is by definition "thinkable." And anything that you choose to think, even if it is scary, nasty, or dangerous, is okay to think about. This is self-acceptance, self-intimacy. There is nothing wrong, for example, with your thinking lustful thoughts about another or of abandoning a responsibility, even of doing harm to another. Inner-liberated persons have learned to think "aloud" to themselves, without self-condemnation. To love the "me" in "you" means that you identify with another person because you see parts of your own humanness, your own strength and weaknesses as a human being, in the other person too. If you have come to accept yourself, to love yourself in spite of your foibles, then it will be infinitely easier to come closer to, to identify with, to love another.

Level-IV intimacy might be all right for short periods of time, but it is generally too intense, too demanding, too stifling, to be sustained over a long period of time. Sharing everything, every thought, every nuance of your existence —inner and outer—would be suffocating. And in the process, both parties would have to compromise much of their personal identities, preventing each from becoming all that it might have been possible for him to become. They would also tend to snuff out those around them. Who can stand do be around two people for very long when they constantly dote on each other? This might not be too difficult for friends, who can leave; but it can be especially difficult for such a couple's children, who come to feel left out. This kind of intimacy, as with most everything else that is carried to an extreme, is no virtue.

By contrast, Level-III intimacy liberates both parties. Many years ago, when I was involved in a clinical internship, I was given a thirteen-year-old client. Therapy was mandated for this youngster by the probation court. As you can imagine, counseling that is mandatory rather than voluntary is much more difficult to undertake inasmuch as the client, who has been required to come, often tends to resist treatment. In those situations, it becomes necessary for the counselor to attempt to win the client's confidence by whatever means possible so that counseling can take place.

Michael, the thirteen-year-old, was particularly resistant. He would not even talk to me for the first four sessions, but instead sat glued to his chair, keeping his head down, his legs crossed.

"Michael," I said at the first session, "say something. I'm a friendly person." But I got absolutely no response for the entire fifty-minute session.

At the supervisory conference, during which cases were discussed, I brought up the fact of this client's staunch resistance. "Don't worry too much about it," my supervisor said. "This sometimes happens. But when it does, the very fact that you are there sometimes makes a contribution. Next time, tell the boy you are there for him, that it is not necessary for him to talk or say anything if he doesn't wish to, but that you are available to listen and care if he decides that he would like to share with you. Then make yourself comfortable and 'just be.' "

During the next session, I made myself much more comfortable with the silence that ensued between Michael and me. "Michael, I'm here. I care for you. Look, I'm here because this is my job. I have to be here. And you're in this room because you've been required by the court to be here too. These are givens, Michael, and as long as we are in this room together each week for fifty minutes, I'm available to be helpful if I can. But don't feel pressured to say anything if you don't want to."

After that talk, I relaxed. I took a comfortable seat by the window and just sat, available but not pressing at all. Michael in the meantime continued to sit, legs crossed, head down. Two more sessions ensued exactly like this, in absolute silence. I would greet Michael, say, "Hello, I'll be here," and we would sit silently for our fifty-minute session together.

"I don't know what you're doing with Michael, Dr. Kushel," his mother said. "But whatever it is, it seems to be working. He's so much easier to get along with since he's been seeing you." Of course I was surprised.

"Oh," I said, unwilling to betray any of the (non)confidences that Michael and I shared during these silent sessions. Then at the fifth session the miracle happened. "Hi, Michael, I'm available," I said, in what had come to be a custom. "Hi," Michael said in return this time, to my utter shock. A therapeutic bond had developed in silence, without pressure. From that point on, I was able to become close with him.

In Level-III intimacy, there is no pressing for total intimacy. If moments of total intimacy (Level IV) come, they come as a natural evolutionary event, not as something forced.

JOHANNA AND RON

Two years ago, a couple, Johanna and Ron, both in their mid-thirties, came to me for marriage counseling. Ron was a marine engineer and Johanna was a homemaker. They had two young boys, aged four and six. Their ten-year marriage was in jeopardy.

Johanna: "I don't know what happened to our relationship. It was so loving, so wonderful. We were very much a part of one another for many, many years." She went on to explain that she had met Ron eleven years ago while they both were working for the same engineering company in Philadelphia. "When we met, it seemed one of those miraculous happenings. You know. The chemistry was just right for the both of us. Perfect compatibility: sexually, intellectually—everything. Ron was always my best friend. And that, combined with a marvelous physical relationship, was my dream of what a great marriage should be, and we really had a lot going for us.

"And that's the way it was, oh, for many years. At least the first six or seven. We would travel before we had children. Europe, Hawaii, whenever we could save up a little money and get the time off. Even when we had our children, we were so close. And Ron was always my closest companion. He looked upon me that way too."

Ron: "That's right. We were extremely close for a long time. There wasn't a thing that I couldn't discuss with Jo. I felt she understood me, appreciated me in a way that no one had ever appreciated me before. I was the same with her, just as she's been saying. We were a team, and a great team at that. It's not that we had to do everything together. Not at all. But we shared everything about what we were thinking and feeling. There wasn't a thing I couldn't talk to Jo about."

Johanna: "Ron would even be able to share his sex fantasies with me—even his thoughts about other women—and I wouldn't get upset."

Ron: "You were very understanding."

Johanna: "But somehow, all that seems to have changed now. We seem to have drifted far apart. Much too far apart. Nothing is the same between us anymore, but why, I'm just not sure. That's why we've come for counseling. We seem to have drifted apart. Something very serious has gone wrong with our marriage and neither of us seems to know what it is—or even how it happened.

"Lately, Ron talks very little with me. He's keeping to himself. And we seem to fight over the smallest incidents. Sometimes we fight over the thermostat. He says it's too hot, and I say it's too cold. Also, we've been having trouble with the kids. Not both of them, but the older one is very active. Hyperactive, I guess is the word. And Ron blames me for not raising him correctly, and I blame him. I think that I could use just a little more help from him as the father. Isn't the father supposed to be the disciplinarian? What happened to the closeness we once had? Now we're more like enemies, not friends."

As I continued counseling with this couple. I learned that Ron had advanced on the job and had had many more opportunities for growth than his wife. They had, indeed, drifted apart.

A fusion of two persons into one is unrealistic and cannot sustain itself. Certainly much that is positive can be said about a relationship that is based on the high levels of openness, sharing, and interdependency that characterized the early years of Johanna and Ron's marriage. Their relationship was predicated upon the "right" but generally quite ineffective idea of a fusion of two spirits into a marvelous kind of oneness—a Level-IV intimacy. Unfortunately, this kind of oneness has great difficulty in sustaining itself over an extended period of time. In those rare cases where a couple has managed this extreme cohesiveness throughout a lifetime, a price is paid in terms of personal autonomy.

Individuality, independence, and a genuine acceptance of his existential aloneness are central aspects of an inner-liberated person's personality. Therefore, to fuse, to integrate, to blend and merge for a long time at Level-IV intimacy, is asking the inner-liberated person to compromise much too much of himself. Level III is quite sufficient and can be much more enduring. It is not that you cannot enjoy the peak experiences that can come from moments of Level-IV intimacy from time to time, but Level-III intimacy provides sufficient opportunity to share what you think and feel. This leaves you open psychological space to be your own person as well.

Two people in love still need plenty of "space" if their love is to endure. Inner-liberated intimacy is not possessive. The following reflects such an attitude: "We can become very, very close, share *almost* everything very deeply as if we are one. Then we can just as easily move apart— he going his way for a while, me going mine. And I really don't want to know all the bloody details of what he does with his time away from me—unless for some reason he wants to share that with me. I don't want to share each and every aspect of my life with him either. There are some parts of my life, as close as we are, that are mine alone. And I like it that way. And he likes it too, I believe."

The initial Level-IV intimacy shared by Johanna and Ron lacked this character. There was too high a level of interdependence. Although they were apparently nourished by each other's presence during the early years of their marriage, they were placing an unreasonable demand upon themselves. If during the early years of their marriage they had made it a point to find exciting dimensions of their life apart from each other, independent of each other, they would in later years not have drifted so far apart. Their tacit understanding would have been, "We share intimately many aspects of our lives, but there is still part of each of us that is for ourselves alone."

A THOUGHT FOR YOUR FILES (CHOOSE ONE)

Defective Thought	Effective Thought
In marriage, two blend into one. $(½+½=1)$	In marriage, I am still me and you are still you, and the marriage is a third entity in our relationship. $(1+1+1[\text{the marriage}]=3)$

It is axiomatic to the inner-liberated way of life that you not surrender yourself totally to another. When you permit yourself to become close, to become intimate, it is not on a completely unconditional basis. There are conditions to the temporary surrender of yourself. There are only certain times and places that you can decide to let yourself go entirely, to permit yourself to become highly dependent, to become fused into the life space of another. These times and places are, realistically, special circumstances rather than a complete way of life.

We can listen to the poet Gibran, who wrote, "You talk when you cease to be at peace with your thoughts." It is in the thoughts that we cannot possibly share that we probably find the deepest levels of peace.

The orgiastic experience, based on a total fusion, is the antithesis of aloneness. According to Erich Fromm, the renowned psychoanalyst, individuals from all cultures pursue orgiastic experiences in one form or another. Certain dances sometime bring natives to orgasm. Certainly high-level physical intimacy culminates in an orgiastic peak. Great experiences in the arts, in music, even in games, can produce an orgiastic response. It is during these peak experiences that we as individuals are released form the isolation of our self and are galvanized, for the moment of orgasm, into a communion, a unity with universal forces larger than self. Orgasm, in a sense, is an escape from loneliness.

You may have observed that many people who suffer "loneliness anxiety," who fear or are incapable of sustaining a genuine and more lasting kind of intimacy (Level III), tend to leap into Level-IV intimacies, hoping against hope to permanently overcome the fundamental aloneness that inner-liberated persons wisely have come to accept and even to appreciate. Ron and Johanna, in their Level-IV intimacy, were victims of a similar trap. Beneath all this need for closeness was a deep fear of being alone.

Drifting apart

It was Ron who was fortunate enough to have done most of the growing in a positive direction. He found his job as a marine engineer challenging and rewarding. He had a sense of progress as he moved up in his company. His work brought him into contact with a wide range of interesting people and permitted him to travel to different parts of the country, adding breadth and depth to his development.

Meanwhile, since the birth of their two children, life was not nearly as expansive for Johanna. As much as one would like to say that homemaking is a creative and challenging job, for many women it represents being trapped. Is it really a wonder that she and Ron drifted apart? Because Johanna had learned to depend on Ron's success as a substitute for creating her own identity, she became a victim.

Conventional thinking suggests that Johanna and Ron begin doing more things together. Find mutual interests. Take a holiday together. Share more. Try to become more intimate again. But that is not at all an inner-liberating train of thought.

Drawing upon inner-liberating principles, I suggested the following to them: Ron should remain caring and available, should continue to grow both on his job and personally. Johanna should develop a specific independent course of action that will enable her to become more free of Ron and psychologically stronger on her own. They should share the less than romantic aspects of household management and childrearing on an equal basis. This meant that Ron would have to table some of his adventures at work. Johanna and Ron should move independently toward inner-liberated lifestyles for themselves.

This course required that they seek intimacy with each other, not at Level IV (their previous level), but at Level III —a more realistic and lasting goal. Let's explore aspects of each of these recommendations in greater detail.

Ron should remain caring and available and should continue to grow. In order to reach a satisfactory level of intimacy with another, it is not necessary that you compromise one iota of your own psychosocial development. At the same time that you are growing, developing, you can lend support to your partner, who more than likely is in a different psychological stage of development. After all, there is no reason to expect that two individuals, no matter how close they might have been at one point, will change at exactly the same time or in the same way. People tend to change in spurts—when the conditions, both external and internal, are ripe. It is difficult to hurry internal clocks. Yet when one person changes, you can be sure that this will have a definite effect on the other, especially if their relationship is a highly dependent one.

At the same time, if you are fortunate enough to be making progress in your life, it is important that you be sensitive to the effects this will have on those who are close to you. There is no need for you to feel guilty for making progress in your life. However, your partner is likely to be upset when she finds that the "buttons" that at one time were guaranteed to move you no longer seem connected. The nuts and bolts in the superstructure that bound you together may very well have loosened. However, you can still be gentle and supportive. In essence, you will be encouraging your partner to become inner-liberated too. You will do all you can to assist her, at the same time recognizing full well that you cannot really take responsibility for what she chooses to think and feel, even though she is very close to you.

Johanna should develop a specific course of action that leads to her own personal growth. An inner-liberated lifestyle is best caught rather than taught. You really can't lecture another person into growth and development. But probably one of the best ways to influence those close to you, to improve their lot, is to improve your own lot. If adopting an inner-liberated way of life improves your existence, as it is likely to do, then that in itself is a gift to others. Seeing you take on a vital life, others might choose to pattern themselves after you.

It is at best difficult to suggest a change in lifestyle to another. Yet your partner, because you have changed, will also need to change. You cannot stop this change from taking place. Johanna had to see to it that she developed whatever resources she could muster toward her own personal growth, independently of Ron. She eventually enrolled in a college program after some clarification of her personal directions.

The sharing of day-to-day chores must be equalized. Household management and childrearing chores must be equally divided. Removing the garbage, settling the checking account, making home repairs, shopping, and supervising the children all take their toll. These are hardly romantic, yet they need to be done. The division of labor becomes an important ingredient in the sustaining of intimacy—a kind of behind-the-scenes work. It is not necessary to tackle these chores strictly along stereotypical sex-role lines. Husband can do the dishes. Wife can repair the plumbing. Husband can feed and diaper. Wife can go to the office. It really does not matter how a couple divides up the work that needs to be done. What matters is that they periodically review their bargain in terms of the work load and check to see that each is holding up his end of the bargain. Conditions change as children grow. Often it becomes necessary to renegotiate the work-load agreement.

Since Johanna found doing the housework and raising the two boys while Ron pursued his career an unsatisfactory arrangement, it became necessary to redistribute the work load. She needed time for her college studies and for her own personal growth. Ron found time to help more with managing the house and children.

Each partner should continue to move toward his own form of inner liberation. Individuality is to be encouraged for both partners. Having unrealistic expectations is one of the reasons why so many marriages are failing. Aiming for a less than perfect intimacy is much more realistic and permits both parties to continue to be separate, whole individuals who come together intimately at certain times but not all the time. In a sense, you are living alone together.

You may share much intimately, yet you still have your own life—a life that you may make as inner-liberated as possible. This means that you may have as satisfying a personal existence as is humanly possible; a life characterized by calm, purpose, and adventure. Such a life can be your number-one priority if you have sufficient space.

It is as if you are swimming pleasurably in a delicious swimming pool and you say to a prospective intimate, "Come on in if you like. The water is wonderful, and there's plenty of space for you here too." It is this kind of intimacy, a nonpossessive, open warmth and willingness to share, that provides for a lasting, enduring relationship.

In the case of Ron and Johanna, Ron was able to assist Johanna after a period of time into a period of growth. Johanna learned to come to terms with the part of herself that was fundamentally alone, and out of this aloneness she was eventually able to find her own genuine purposes, which included loving relationships for her children and for Ron, but also her search for deeper expression. Her college courses became increasingly important to her.

With Johanna and Ron both moving along toward their own forms of inner liberation, the pressure for a "successful relationship" eased considerably. It subsequently became possible for both of them to easily weather periods when the relationship was not doing all that well. In their eyes, it was possible for them to tolerate a poor relationship for short periods of time and still continue to have a most satisfying personal existence. The way they came to view their moments of Level-IV intimacy was as a bonus, a fringe benefit, not a way of life. They learned to appreciate Level-III intimacy as a way of life instead.

SEXUAL INTIMACY

Thus far we have been discussing psychological intimacy. Sexual and psychological intimacy go hand in hand. But some focus upon the sheer physical aspects of intimacy is worthy of attention too. What I am talking about, of course, is sex, intercourse, "the making of love."

I mentioned Desmond Morris' book, *Intimacy,* and how he divides physical intimacy into a sequence of twelve distinct progressive steps. The first is eye-to-body contact, the second is eye-to-eye contact. Subsequent steps lead to greater intimacy. The middle stages include such contact as arm to shoulder, arm to waist, etc. The more advanced steps of intimacy are hand to genital, and finally genital to genital—considered by Morris as the height of physical intimacy. However, he quickly points out that sexual intimacy doesn't always follow this sequence. In sex one might move toward the tenth, eleventh, or even the twelfth steps, then only later take a look, eye to eye.

Biologically, it is possible for us to be attracted physically —genital to genital—to more than one person over the course of a lifetime. However, social convention and sheer practicality dictate that it is neither possible nor wise to be physically intimate with everyone that you would hypothetically like to have sex with. Although inner-liberated persons are lively, lustful, energetic, and sensual, they have at their disposal the means for maintaining their social and psychological equilibrium with this sometimes complicating condition. Since they learn to use their imaginations effectively, they are able to comfortably masturbate when necessary. Their lively imaginations also help them sustain a very high quality of intercourse with their partners. By choosing the necessary effective thoughts, they learn how to overcome many of the sexual problems that plague others.

Many so-called sexual problems are caused by choosing defective thoughts. Some of the more common problems "cured" by effective thoughts include premature ejaculation, impotency, vaginismus, unhappiness over the lack of variety, and fear of experimenting with new techniques, all of which are caused in a large part, by defective thinking. An account of how one of my clients cured himself of premature ejaculation will serve to illustrate how choosing more effective thoughts can "remedy" sexual problems.

Stewart, a twenty-nine-year-old lawyer who had been married for four years, came to me for counseling, complaining of a sense of deep depression and a gnawing sense of worthlessness. After several sessions he spoke openly about a sexual problem that he had had for many years that was connected with his feelings of worthlessness: "Ever since I was a teenager, whenever I was about to make out with a woman, I would end up spraying all over myself. I must have ruined twenty-five pairs of pants with my own sperm. This wasn't too much of a problem for me before I got married, but now that I've been married for over four years, I've come to realize it's become a very serious problem. Especially for my wife, Ann. I know that I don't sustain an erection long enough to satisfy her—even though she's never complained. I'm a thirty-second man at best, and I feel damned ashamed about it. It wasn't too bad before I was married. But now that I'm married I want to do something about it."

Stewart learned how to choose the necessary thoughts that permitted him to sustain an erection for longer than he originally thought was possible. Here's how he did it:

Having put himself into a trance by using the auto-suggestion technique, he suggested to his subconscious mind that he would last and last when having sex. He visualized going through all of the stages of making love with his wife—from the first touch through all the latter stages. He was able to visualize clearly the moment of penetration and even to experience the identical bodily sensations that usually brought him to orgasm. However he practiced, in his mind's eye, accepting these exciting stimuli without orgasm. He visualized himself just going on and on, thrusting for at least fifteen minutes. He imagined that he experimented with new positions, enriching the experience both for his wife and for himself, all without succumbing to ejaculation.

After all this, he, in his imagination, permitted himself to totally let go—to have a strong, animalistic, fully explosive orgiastic experience. Of course during the self-hypnosis, Stewart was able to choose whether he wanted to bring himself to full orgasm. If he did, it was labeled masturbation. However, once the imagery of successful intercourse without prematurely coming was clearly embedded in his subconscious mind, he had an awareness of what was possible for him.

He now had an achievable ideal toward which he could move. It was a full six months before, according to Stewart's account, he could put successfully into practice all that he had taught himself. But at the conclusion of our work together, Stewart reported total success.

This, in conjunction with mastering other aspects of inner-liberated living, set Stewart on a course for overcoming much of the sense of despair and feelings of worthlessness that he had been experiencing at the outset. The important point is that it was Stewart's effective thoughts that brought about his eventual remediation.

Our taste in faces, temperament, even body types, is one that is a result of years and years of conditioning. Your response to breasts, lips, hair, eye movement, are not all physical. You were inadvertantly *taught* to respond the way that you do. If your partner has a peculiar personality trait, or a twitch, a mole—superfluous hair on some part of the body—you can easily recondition yourself to be more accepting. You can choose effective thoughts such as "hair on the arms no longer irritates me" and reprogram your subconscious. Certainly most tastes that we have have come about through conditioning. For example, in certain European countries it is considered vulgar for women to shave their legs, yet in the United States, that is a common practice. It is the inner self of the person you pair yourself with that has the most significant bearing on the quality of your relationship. And it is the closeness of your inner self with the inner self of another that creates the highest levels of intimacy.

In general, then, inner-liberating intimacy provides space for the parties to still be individuals. Although they often enjoy moments of intense closeness, they realize that Level-IV intimacy is usually too intense to be sustained over a long period of time.

Chapter
· 11 ·
Risking

He that leaveth nothing to
chance will do few things
ill, but he will do very few things.

—Lord Halifax

When Marc took the receiver off the hook, his heart began to pound like that of an adolescent. He could hardly breathe. "This is too much," he thought. He put down the receiver, took a handkerchief from his pocket, and wiped the clammy sweat from his forehead and both palms. "Imagine," he thought, "a grown man afraid to make a call, to risk failure, to experience rejection."

Alice used to enjoy her work, but now more and more was being piled on her already overloaded desk. It seemed as if there was no way out. She was tired of being "dumped on," literally and figuratively, but she just didn't seem able to muster up the courage to put a stop to it.

"Look at this awful traffic jam," Hank lamented. For years now, he had been fantasizing a time when he would turn his car off the crowded expressway some morning and not show up for work. He dreamed of heading for the beach, taking a swim, wandering carefree along the shore. But no. Good old reliable Hank. They could always count on good old Hank, veritable prisoner of his own reliable reputation.

Taking risks is an integral part of an inner-liberated way of life. The synergy of calm, purpose, and adventure enables one to engage in and enjoy risk-taking ventures with little of the anxiety that most other people experience in similar circumstances. Inner-liberated persons generally take a low-tension approach to most risking, risking that most people find energy draining, and so are able to conserve their energy for the times when it may actually be needed.

Life with surprise in it has zest. Perhaps that is one of the reasons why reading the morning newspaper remains such a popular pastime. People are curious to see if something new has happened in the world overnight. But this is often insufficient. There can be a wearisome sameness in the headlines, the stockmarket, even the ballgame scores. Vicarious excitement, though helpful, is not enough. People yearn for more adventure in their lives, but day-after-day routine is all they often have.

Some kinds of risks might seem well worth taking. Others, quite foolish, even stupid. Mindless, thrill-seeking behavior might serve as an occasional respite from responsible living. However, the kinds of risk taking that we will focus upon in this chapter will be of a more purposeful nature. We will examine calculated risks that tend to lead toward greater inner liberation, a more satisfying personal existence.

The Four Essential Steps Toward Effective Risk Taking

Effective risk taking requires that the prospective risk taker go through four necessary steps usually, but not always, in this sequence:

(1) Assess the prospects for success.

(2) Imagine handling effectively the worst that could possibly happen in the event of failure.

(3) Imagine completing the risk in ideal fashion.

(4) Keeping the positive fantasy in mind, let go, act, and enjoy.

1: *Assessing the prospects for success.* Even risks that are taken on short notice require forethought. Remember the cartoon of a sad sack character jumping head first into an empty swimming pool? Ouch! Check out the situation in advance as soon as possible. Have some sense of the odds you face. All risks should be calculated to some extent. Decide if the reward involved seems worth the risk involved. If it does, then proceed to step two.

2: *Imagining that you are handling effectively the worst that could happen in the event of failure.* Can you handle the prospect of failure? Can you afford to lose? Sometimes an individual becomes aware that the stakes in case of loss are overwhelming. For example if you were to fail to pass a speeding car on a narrow highway and a crash proved inevitable, the loss would be considerable—perhaps your life and even the lives of others. However, given sufficient space and time, you might venture the risk. But failure, in this instance, would be irreconcilable and unconscionable.

However, with a great number of other risks, the ways of dealing with the possibility of failure are multifold. It is often possible to invent a large number of effective approaches for dealing with failure. If, for example, one were to approach a stranger and attempt to engage him in conversation, imagine the worst that could happen. If the advances were ignored, would the risk taker pass out? Would he cry? In either case, the risk taker will survive. If he passes out in his imagination, what then? He can imagine getting up off the ground, when he regains consciousness and going about his business. In fact anything that he imagines, short of bodily harm, can be handled in the mind's eye if approached creatively.

This step is one that is often omitted by those who too quickly urge people to risk by thinking only positive thoughts. Then the possibility of failure seems to lurk ominously in the back of the risk taker's mind and is often blown far out of proportion to the risk taker's capacity to handle it. It is precisely at this stage that inner-liberated persons are most inventive. And it is this process, thinking through the possibility of failure, that allows them to engage in low-tension risking when others experience great anxiety in the same situation.

3: Imagining completing the risk in ideal fashion. Our images serve as our self-fulfilling prophecies. Therefore, it is worthwhile for the risk taker to take the time to imagine a positive picture of completing the task in an *ideal* fashion. This takes practice and concentration, but the benefits derived are well worth the effort. Some do this quite instinctively. Recently, the world's high-jump record was broken by a young man who attested that he saw in his mind's eye a vivid picture of himself successfully jumping over the crossbar—moments before he turned it into an actuality.

4: Keeping the positive fantasy in mind, let go, act, and enjoy. Keeping the positive image clearly in mind, let go of everything else. Let go of appraising. It's too late for that now. Let go of failing. It's far too late to think of any of that now. Let go of everything except the positive feeling of yourself succeeding. At this moment you are really doing it. You are acting. R-I-S-K. You give to this venture just what is needed. You have what it takes. You are enjoying. You have risked.

Application

It is a very close tennis match. It's your second serve. If your serve goes in, you can tie up the game. If it goes out, you lose. Tension.

Appraising the risk. Not too much choice here. You're

already involved in the game, and you probably are not going to choose to walk off the court. However, the real question of risk centers around whether you should serve hard, trying for a winner. Or should you play it safely with a gentle second serve? You evaluate your opponent and decide that you can reasonably risk going for broke since your serve can sometimes be quite strong and you think that you can catch him by surprise.

Thinking through the worst. All that can happen to you, you figure, is that you could lose the game. That is a lot, but you also figure that you won't be destroyed if you lose. Oh, your opponent might heckle you a bit and you might also berate yourself for a short time, but in no case does missing this point imply total disaster. You find this realization quite comforting. So, you think, calming yourself, "All this isn't quite as bad as it seemed at first." If you can survive the worst that you can imagine, then there is little to really worry about.

Imagining a beautiful, strong serve right to your opponent's weak side. A winner. You fix this very positive image of hitting this marvelous serve clearly in your mind's eye. You can almost taste it.

Holding on clearly to the positive picture imprinted in your mind (a resounding serve), you move into action. You let go of all reservation, all appraising, all fear. You act out the image in your mind's eye. You act. You R-I-S-K. You give just what it takes—no more, no less. And you enjoy the excitement of the risk.

Good going. I hope that it went in for a winner. If you fully concentrated and applied these four steps exactly as described, your chances for success were excellent.

LOW-TENSION RISKING

There are occasions when nothing can adequately reduce the tension of a particular risk, such as when the odds are really against you and the goal is of special importance.

However, there are thoughts you can choose that can make even the most intimidating of risks less frightening. The train of thought that Max employed illustrates this.

Max, in his early thirties, married, with two small children, sought counseling because he had very little confidence in himself even though he was employed as an office manager for a large insurance company and appeared to those who didn't know him well to be "up and coming."

Asking for a raise can be extremely nerve-wracking, especially if your colleagues have warned you that the boss doesn't like to be pressed and has been known to fire employees for less. When jobs are scarce and one has a wife and two young children depending upon the paychecks, it is even more difficult. Max did risk asking for a raise; the following reflects the inner-liberating line of thought he finally developed to minimize his anxiety.

"No, I didn't get very uptight asking for the raise. First of all, I figured out that they [the company] had enough money in the till so that they could afford to give me a justified increase. I was aware that they knew damn well that I was doing good work. So I personally figured that my prospects were quite good regardless of what the crowd said.

"Secondly, the way I figured it, what's the worst thing that could happen to me if the boss didn't like my asking? Fire me? Right! He definitely wouldn't hit me. I knew that he couldn't put me in jail. The worst that he could do was fire me. So then I figured, okay, so if he fires me, what then? I thought about that for quite a while.

"The way I've come to feel about myself these days is that although I really like working there, it's not the only job that I can do in order to make a living. Hell, if I had to, I believe that I could do landscaping, selling, even factory work. So with that in mind, I said to myself, 'Max, what have you got to be scared of?' However, then I thought of Cheryl and the kids. What about them? After all, they count on my paycheck every two weeks, and I wouldn't want to let them down by losing this job.

"So here's the way that I handled that. I said to myself, 'Max, Cheryl loves you for what you are, not for the fact that you're a big-deal office manager and bringing home a check every two weeks. And if she doesn't really love you for what you are, then this is as good a time as ever to find out. So I figured, I'm not afraid of the truth; whatever the truth is, I can handle it. This led me to the conclusion that the risk of asking for the raise could only lead toward a clearer picture of reality. It would help me get closer to the truth about my marriage, possibly, and I was certainly bound to find out whether I really have any kind of future with this company. Anyhow, asking was my goal. I figured I had a fighting chance. If I didn't get it, I could still handle any of the consequences. So, I went in—and I asked. And I got it."

Analysis of Max's thinking

Max's risk taking freed him to put into effect other inner-liberating concepts. The playing of roles as compared to actually doing a job was a central concept in his line of thought. Max was clearly able to tell the difference between playing roles and real action. He alluded to his comprehension of this concept when he said, "They knew damn well that I was doing good work." Max believed that he was actually doing a job for the company rather than merely playing a role.

Playing a role is similar to being in a play or show. You look as if you are real, but you are actually pretending. Many persons confuse role-playing with the real thing. Inner-liberated persons do not. Max also concerned himself with this important principle when he reflected on his wife, Cheryl. "If she doesn't love me for what I am, then this is as good a time as ever to find out." If Cheryl was simply playing the role of wife and lover, he would find this out if his risk-taking venture were to fail. Max perceived Cheryl as a true friend and lover, not simply a person playing the conventional role of wife, and he was willing to find out if his perceptions were correct. He was not limited to basing his thoughts only on illusion, but on actual behavior.

Inner-liberated persons are not above playing roles, but they also do jobs, and they clearly know the difference between the two. They see role-playing for what it is and do not take "playing" seriously. They take the jobs they (and other people) do, quite seriously, because doing a job is real and role-playing is not.

Imagine a man with a white jacket and a stethoscope. He stands ominously in front of you, dangling his stethoscope. He says, "I'm a physician—an important physician." "Great," you say, "but can you heal people? What's your healing average?" And he replies, "Can't you see? This is a stethoscope, and a doctor's jacket. I'm a doctor!" "Yes," you respond, calmly, "but can you heal? What's your batting average?" And the man in the doctor's outfit walks away, disgusted with you.

There are many people walking around with the trappings of a role who cannot perform at all when it comes to a test. I once knew a person who was a lifeguard. He was tall and tanned, and he looked very competent sitting high up in his lifeguard's chair at the beach. Thank goodness no one needed his help that summer, for he confided to me one evening that he couldn't swim for more than five strokes before sinking.

All of us are required by society to play a variety of roles each day, and there is nothing inherently wrong with that, as long as we don't confuse roles with reality.

Max's reference to his new attitude was clarified by his subsequent comments. He confided to me that his father had dominated him for most of his life and that he had only recently confronted his father about that fact. After the blowup, Max said he felt emancipated from needing to please his father, the way he had for so long. This difficult and painful experience led Max to a low period in which he succeeded in redefining himself in his current fashion.

Many of the other persons that I have come to identify as inner-liberated noted that they also experienced a similar period of despair in which they learned to develop a more effective definition of themselves. Such a period of despair can be the result of taking a risk and not succeeding, but what separates inner-liberated persons from the rest is that they bounce back and are inspired to redefine themselves. Very often when a person survives a difficult period he emerges all the stronger, and the resources and new perspectives developed out of such a situation can often have long-lasting positive effects. That's been my experience too.

Certainly, if I had not gone into a period of despair after I was rejected for the dean's job years ago, I never would have made all the personal discoveries I did about inner liberation since then.

The degree of caring is another factor worth considering here. Max was certainly a caring person, even if he appeared to others to have "nerves of steel." He cared about his wife and his children. He cared about his job. He cared about getting a raise. And he also cared about himself. Caring about oneself is often misconstrued as selfishness. Self-care is not the same as selfishness. Selfishness suggests caring about yourself regardless of what happens to other persons. Inner-liberated persons are not selfish but do exercise a great deal of self-care. They identify with all of mankind, yet they realize that if they are not in pretty good shape they will have very little of consequence that they can offer others.

Not caring about what others think or do is usually a glib simplification. "I don't care," can usually be more accurately translated, "I don't care as much about_____ _____as I do about_____or_____. But I care more about_____than I do about_____ or_____." Max cared about his job, about his wife and children, about the raise. But it was all a matter of degree. The fact that inner-liberated persons have ordered their lives' priorities prepares them for situations such as this.

Marilyn, a thirty-three-year-old executive with two small children, came to me for counseling about three years ago. She was recently divorced. She rapidly learned how to overcome the tension that often accompanies being alone in social situations by choosing effective lines of thought. Marilyn enjoyed attending many functions that were traditionally reserved for couples or groups, and it was her inner-liberated point of view that provided her with pleasure in situations where she formerly experienced embarrassment and tension.

"At first, when I had just been divorced, I was terrified to do anything alone. I had become so dependent on Bill, and let's face it, life in the suburbs is definitely couple oriented. Oh, I guess I was always able to enjoy kicking my shoes off around my apartment alone. But to go out to a first-class restaurant alone, or even a movie—not on your life. I just wasn't brought up that way. However, I've learned a lot about life since my divorce, and I have really changed for the better. I don't know if people who see me at the theater on a Saturday night really think to themselves, 'Look at that poor soul, all alone, and on Saturday night no less!' I don't know if they do, but if they do, at least I don't preoccupy myself very much with what they might be thinking. Somehow it's become a whole lot less important to me as to whether other people are thinking about me or not. I have enough trouble taking responsibility for what I think. There's nothing that I can do about what other people think.

"Anyhow, I actually enjoy going out alone these days. In fact, I've had some of the most exciting times of my life by myself. Don't misunderstand, sharing with another person has its own pleasures; I appreciate that. But being alone has its unique advantages, too. It's an important dimension to my life.

"Take last night. I treated myself to a most elegant dinner in the finest restaurant in town—all by myself. And I really had a wonderful time. The place was filled with couples and groups, but I'm beyond having that interfere with my personal pleasure. I relished a delicious lobster, a good wine—all to a backdrop of soft dinner music. Sheer pleasure. Everything was perfection. And I tasted, slowly, at my own deliberate pace, every morsel. I paid no attention to some of the stares I received from some of the people there. I can't be responsible for their experiences, only my own. In the truest sense, I was not out alone. I was having a pleasureable experience with a very dear friend. Me."

Analysis of Marilyn's thinking

Marilyn had really learned to utilize and appreciate her own sensory experiences and was not overly concerned about what other persons might be thinking about her. She took full responsibility for herself and did, it seems, quite well on her own behalf. She knew how to enjoy her present moments and apparently respected herself sufficiently to feel lovable. She was able to have a very positive experience in a situation where many persons would have an anxious, even unpleasant, nerve-wracking time. Marilyn is determined, of course, to have a very satisfying personal existence.

She did not have a sour grapes attitude toward the people who were with others, appreciating that there are significant values in being with others as well. Instead, she simply understood that she was having a different kind of venture. It was not necessarily better, and it certainly was not worse. It was just different. The idea of going out with a very dear friend, yourself, is one you should consider.

There are risks that are not consciously viewed as risks. For example, a person is sometimes thought of as very independent when in reality he is just afraid to ask for help. "Independent" is often a cover for fear of risking rejection or looking foolish.

Donna, a risk taker, looked at asking for help this way: "When I ask if I can borrow my neighbor's car once in a while, she can always say no if she wants to. I won't get upset if she says no. In fact I deeply feel that she is entitled to say no if that's what she wants to say. I don't feel as if I can take responsibility for her situation any more than I can expect that she can take responsibility for mine. So I went over to see her yesterday and said, 'Linda, can I borrow your car for a little while to go to the store? My car is being fixed. Okay?' Well, she looked at me kind of funny, then kind of reluctantly she gave me the keys. I really appreciated her lending me the car. I really needed it. Where I live, you're absolutely at a loss without one. I knew that I would be glad to do the same for her if the situation were reversed. Now I know that she didn't seem particularly happy lending it to me. But she did it anyhow. And I'm very glad that she did. And if she didn't, I still would not have taken it as especially personal. I honestly feel that she's entitled to make her own decision. I just would have tried someone else in the neighborhood. People are often glad to help out if you just ask. Now don't get me wrong. I'm not out to make a pest of myself or use other people. I value people too much for that. The way I look at it, when I ask them for help, in a way I'm giving them a chance to find out more about themselves and what they really feel. I just hope that they can be honest with me."

Men who act overly macho are often afraid of risking to ask for help. So are students who are afraid to raise their hands in class and ask about something that they do not quite understand. "Everyone will find out that I'm stupid." Ted, an eighteen-year-old high school student and former client, developed an interesting rationale for asking questions: "Many of my friends are so concerned with how they look that they actually pretend that they know what is going on in science class. They almost never ask questions, even when they don't know what Mr. Kaufman is talking about. It seems that I'm always the one. So when Kaufman explains something and he uses a few words that I've never heard before, my hand goes up. Everyone else is just sitting there pretending that they know what it is that he's talking about. So Kaufman gives me that big fisheye of his—and then he clarifies what it is that he's talking about. Hell, I just want to learn science; I'm not into impressing Kaufman. Then after class, it happens every time, somebody'll come up to me and say, 'Boy, I didn't understand that either, but am I glad that it was you that asked him to explain it.' Listen, that's the way a lot of people are, I know it. But I can't take responsibility for them. It's hard enough just taking responsibility for myself."

Mistaken attitudes toward risk takers sometimes inhibit those who should know better from doing what is in their best interest in the long run. The inner-liberated approach to risk taking sometimes requires that we discount popular opinion in favor of effective thinking.

WORTHY RISKS

Inner-liberated persons sometimes do engage in high-tension risks. But then you can be sure that the risks are worthwhile. An artist undertaking a new form of painting, for example, sometimes sets up such a risk. Art has its own internal logic, and the painter faces problems that he might never have had to face if he hadn't tried a new form of painting.

Reaching out beyond familiar and established boundaries in any area can often be an intensive risk-taking venture but highly worthwhile, as is shown in the case of Alma, a forty-year-old client whose purposes allowed her greater risking. She played the roles of wife, mother, and high-school teacher well, but her primary definition of herself was derived from none of these. She valued herself most as a serious composer of important music. Her musical compositions seemed to add a powerful dimension to her existence, as if she were in communion with some deeper aspect of life. She puts it this way:

"I get something very special out of writing my music. I don't know exactly what it is. At least I can't seem to convey what it is with just words. I suppose the music just speaks for itself. It has a language all of its own. What I do know is that my music is a passion for me. I love working on it, and I'm preoccupied with it a good portion of my time, even though I might not write anything significant more than once or twice in a whole year.

"I'm always working on one piece or another, even at faculty meetings. In fact, almost always at faculty meetings. They're so blessed boring that if I didn't have my music to work on, I don't know what I'd do. That's one of the things that I value most about this; working on it is so portable. I can take it most anywhere—while waiting in line at the post office, cooking, even while driving to work in the morning. Then people wonder why I'm so easygoing and don't seem to get annoyed with some of the seemingly onerous obligations we all seem to get caught up in these days. Why, they'd feel the same way as I do if they had something going for themselves as I do with my music.

"Of course, it's not all pleasure. As I said, it's a passion with me. So that makes it more than just a hobby. I'm much too serious about it to call it a hobby. I do it mainly for me and no one else. Oh, if someone were to enjoy or appreciate what I'm composing, then I'd consider it a bonus, but actually I do it primarily for my own benefit. Not that it is all joy. In fact, I'm a little bit compulsive about it; and I always seem to be creating new problems with my work. I'm always trying to surpass myself, and it's a very big challenge. I find this whole creative process absolutely fascinating. And it's when I'm reaching out beyond myself that I really know that I'm risking. But it's a risk worth taking—and I can call the shots whenever I want to."

Analysis of Alma's thinking

Alma's position was clearly constructed upon a deep and passionate search for meaning. She found that her passion for creating her own musical compositions kept her from being overwhelmed by the many other demands that were made upon her as wife, mother, and teacher. The pleasure she was able to derive from working on her music, even at faculty meetings, is well worth noting. Because her passion was "so portable," as she put it, she was able to extract a good deal of pleasure in situations that tend to alienate or frustrate many other persons.

Alma was fortunate, of course, mainly because she apparently knew what it was that she liked (or needed) to do. Writing original music is not for everyone. But I believe there is some significant talent locked inside almost every person.

The one question that remains is this: Who can determine whether Alma's music is any good if she doesn't have it performed publicly? Is it sufficiently satisfying for a creator of something to act as sole judge of its worth? Inner-liberated persons such as Alma answer with a resounding Yes. They enjoy as much as anyone else having their work valued, but they don't insist upon it. Alma did share some of her musical work, and when someone did value it, she considered that a marvelous bonus. She put it this way:

"I do it to please myself, mainly. If another person comes to enjoy it too, then of course I'm delighted. But I didn't, to be honest with you, write it for them. I wrote it for me."

Alma had studied music and found that it had its own internal logic and problems of its own. She was connecting into something that goes far beyond everyday existence, it was this connection that gave her the capacity to enjoy day-to-day existence in an extremely satisfying way.

SUMMING UP

Four steps toward effective risk taking were presented and explored. The steps are: 1) appraise the odds; 2) imagine handling the worst in good form; 3) imagine carrying out the risk in question in ideal fashion; and 4) keeping the positive image of the previous step clearly in mind, let go of all else and act. Enjoy. Succeed.

The cases and lines of thought of both Max and Marilyn demonstrated how the degree of tension common to many risk-taking situations can be very much reduced or even eliminated entirely. Max chose a series of thoughts for himself that not only led to attaining a raise but kept him free from the trap of taking roles that he "played" too seriously. He turned a potentially nerve-wracking experience into another inner-liberating event in his life. Marilyn, through her special inner-liberated line of reasoning, was enabled to turn a potentially tension-filled experience into a very pleasant event. Dining out alone without preoccupation about what other people might be thinking about her allowed her the freedom to have a marvelous personal experience. Marilyn had learned to be alone in her own company in a crowd and enjoy it.

Asing for help, whether borrowing your neighbor's car or asking questions in school, is often misconstrued as a sign of weakness. Yet as the inner-liberated persons cited in this chapter testified, it isn't really a weakness but a strength.

Finally, Alma, in her purposeful search for meaning through music, showed how such a search also freed her from taking her other roles too seriously. And she was able to cheerfully function as wife, mother, and teacher because of her more serious and passionate pursuit in composing music. She took her most intense risks with her music and through this, had a much greater control of all other aspects of her day-to-day existence.

Through the process of effective risk taking, coupled with creative inner-liberating lines of thought, a person can really enjoy the challenge of life.

Chapter
·12·
The Real World:
Staying Centered

C ongratulations. You've definitely paved the way for taking on that very satisfying life you promised yourself at the outset. Having taken all six centering steps on the path to inner liberation and having thoroughly familiarized yourself with the applications of this method to real-life situations, you are well on your way to inner liberation.

But wait. Before you congratulate yourself too enthusiastically, there's still one last process that needs attention: keeping your gains and learning how to stay centered in this world.

KEEPING YOUR GAINS

Our world is not always kindly disposed to inner liberation. So many people are fearful. So many are straining to get by each day. So many are filled with "busyness," with the fear of dealing with loneliness, frantically seeking pastimes to avoid the real issues, pressing too hard to "succeed," to be happy, to acquire more and more.

Therefore, you can hardly blame them if they resent and try to modify your attitude, your easy, enjoyable, and exciting way of life. "After all," they say, "that's not supposed to be the way it is. Life is supposed to be hard, difficult, tension filled. Nothing worthwhile comes easily." If you're not careful, you might forget the truth and buy this unfortunate myth once again yourself. Don't let that happen.

After you've launched your new inner-liberated lifestyle, keep a very low profile. Don't make any proud announcements, any great declarations of autonomy. Just quietly go about your personal revolution, low-key, confidently, but with no fanfare. Eventually, after living in inner-liberated fashion becomes a more deeply rooted habit for you, you might venture sharing with others what it is that you are doing.

But even then it will be wise to proceed cautiously for two very good reasons. You will not want to upset too much those who have come to depend upon you as you were, and until these principles are very deeply ingrained in your mind and put into action at least several times around, you can easily let them slip from your grasp. After all, you have no organization to fall back on. Inner liberation is no cult. You have only yourself and your thoughts to rely upon.

You must force yourself into the habit of thinking about what effective thoughts you can choose to make your life more satisfying when things seem to get momentarily out of whack.

A CHECKLIST TO GET YOU RECENTERED

Whenever you find that your inner-liberated way of life, the more satisfying personal existence you've vowed to have, seems to be slipping away from you, review the following checklist to recenter your life:

(1) Have you reminded yourself that your prime purpose in life is to have as satisfying a life as is humanly possible?

(2) Have you permitted yourself to think "he, she, it, or they made me feel this way" instead of taking responsibility for choosing?

(3) Have you reminded yourself "who you really are" at the inner-self level?

(4) Are you aware of the *defective* thoughts you've been choosing?

(5) Have you decided upon the *effective* thoughts you'd rather choose?

(6) Are you, then, regularly choosing these effective thoughts in place of the defective thoughts?

(7) Have you employed the go-along (John Wayne to the rescue) technique to help you catch up with and take charge of unwanted feelings?

(8) Have you scrupulously been avoiding taking triple penalties?

(9) Have you asked yourself the three calming questions recently?

(10) Have you reminded yourself of the inner-liberating personality traits you've acquired to enjoy calm, purpose, and adventure: lovable? open? loving? capable? spontaneous? sensual? others?

(11) Have you reviewed your effective-thought file and reminded yourself of the appropriate facts of life regarding your feelings?

(12) If you've checked all of the above, have you applied autosuggestion to deal with recurring defective thoughts? Have you prepared in advance the effective thoughts you intend to implant in your subconscious, in place of the defective thought(s) that are keeping you from being your inner-liberated self?

(13) Have you reviewed the Inner Liberation Self-Test (Chapter 4) to see where you might be falling short?

(14) Consider attending and all-day Centering Seminar to help you reinforce and supplement the principles that you have learned in this book. If you are interested in attending such a seminar (it's possible to arrange one in your area), please write to Dr. Gerald Kushel, Box 76, Huntington Station, New York, N.Y. 11747 for additional information.

After trying all of the above, successful recentering to your inner-liberating ways can be expected. If you forget to remind yourself that it is your own thoughts and not things outside of you that are are making you feel or act in a less than satisfaying way, then you can easily slip back into employing your old defense mechanisms. And you know full well where that leads: to the surrender of self-responsibility and all the inner-liberating freedoms that you've so recently learned to attain and enjoy.

Appendix

Autosuggestion Script for Progressive Relaxation

Directions: *read text slowly into a cassette tape recorder. Pauses (marked in italics) are for about six seconds. Find a quiet place and a comfortable position before beginning. Use recorded scripts as needed.*

Phase I: Autosuggestion Script for Progressive Relaxation

"Shut your eyes and listen carefully to these instructions.

"You are going to move comfortably and gradually into a very relaxed, peaceful state. Now make the small muscles of your eyelids tense. *(Pause)* Now relax them. Let all of the tension ease out of your eyelids. Now tense up your forehead. *(Pause)* Now let your forehead relax completely. Let all of the tension ease out of your forehead. *(Pause)* That's very good. Now your eyes and forehead are very much at ease, very calm. *(Pause)* Now experience the muscles in your mouth and throat. Be aware of the tiny muscles in your mouth and throat and now let them relax also. *(Pause)* Let your upper jaw and lower jaw separate ever so slightly. That's right. Permit your head and face and jaws to get very, very relaxed. That's very good. *(Pause)* And now experience your right shoulder. *(Pause)* Let it relax. *(Pause)* And now your left shoulder. *(Pause)* Same thing. Let it relax completely. *(Pause)* And now permit yourself to get more and more tired. You are allowing yourself to get more and more tired. *(Pause)* And now experience your spine. *(Pause)* Let it relax completely. Let it go completely limp. *(Pause)* That's fine. You are feeling very confident and trusting, and you know that your suggestions are very helpful, very caring. So you can relax even more now. *(Pause)*

"Now every time you take a breath, imagine that you are breathing in airs of relaxation, airs of complete relaxation. And so when you breathe airs of relaxation in, hold them inside of you for a few moments, and then imagine that you are breathing airs of tension out. Remember, relaxation in, tension out. All right, breathe in airs of relaxation slowly. *(Pause)* Now hold the airs of relaxation for a moment; that's right. Then let all tension out. *(Pause)* Now remember— with each breath, relaxation in and tension out—each time that you breathe. *(Pause)* Now experience your buttocks and then let your buttocks relax. *(Pause)* Your right leg. *(Pause)* And now let your right leg relax also. *(Pause)* Your left leg. *(Pause)* Experience it, then let it relax completely. *(Pause)* Now let your entire body relax. *(Pause for a few moments)* Very good. Remember, relaxation airs in, hold, then all tension out. *(Read very slowly)* Now you are very much at ease, very, very calm."

(This completes the relaxation phase of autosuggestion.)

Phase II: Autosuggestion Script for Moving into Direct Contact with Your Subconscious Mind

Directions: *before recording the next script, read the entire text. You will find that you are asked to imagine yourself going slowly down an escalator. If you have an aversion to going downward, please change all references to "down" and "downward" into "up" and "upward." Do this before you begin to record.*

"Now imagine a large blackboard with big letters on it, spelling out the word 'relax.' In big letters see: R E L A X. *(Pause)* Relax and see this board clearly now. Now, if any extraneous thoughts come into your mind, just let them disappear by having this blackboard with the word "relax" appear in place of them. Now you are quite relaxed and at ease, and you will be moving into an even deeper state where you will be able to communicate directly with your own subconscious.

"In your imagination, now, picture an escalator that is going slowly down, down. You are watching the escalator as it is moving slowly and safely down, into an area of great peace and comfort. A beautiful place of peace and comfort. Imagine such a place, a beautiful, comfortable place. *(Pause)* That's where the escalator is taking you. Now you will begin to count backwards from ten to one, and when you reach number one, you will have arrived at that beautiful, comfortable place you imagined. Now, permit yourself to see the escalator very clearly and now you are getting on it and moving safely down, down, down. Okay. Ten, you are now on the escalator moving gently, slowly. *(Pause)* Nine, you are going down, slowly. Relax. Remember, relaxation as you breathe in, tension is all out. Eight, allow yourself to get sleepier and sleepier. *(Pause)* Now let your whole body become very tired. *(Pause)* Seven, sleepier and sleepier. More and more tired. *(Pause)* Your whole body is extremely heavy now as you go down and down, deeper and deeper, sleepier and sleepier. *(Pause)* Six, you are almost halfway there now—where you will be able to be in a very beautiful, comfortable state, where you will be in a deep, trancelike state. Five, you are at the halfway point now. You can rest completely now if you want to. You are very tired. Very peaceful. And you are very much at ease. *(Pause)* Going down deeper and deeper on the escalator. Four, very sleepy, very tired now. *(Pause)* Getting very close to the bottom. Three, very close to the bottom now where you can sleep. Where you can be in a deep, trancelike state. *(Pause)* Two, you are now sleepier than you have ever been in your entire life and in a moment you will be in a very deep trance. *(Pause)* One, you are in a deep trance now. You have arrived at the place of complete comfort that you imagined earlier. *(Pause)* Experience comfort. Enjoy being here. *(Pause)* You are in a comfortable, trancelike state now—and ready to speak directly to your subconscious. Now first, you will try to open your eyes in one moment, but you will not be able to open them. You will try, but no matter how hard you try, you will not be able to open your eyes.

"All right, now try to open your eyes. You cannot open them because you are going along with the suggestion that you cannot. *(Pause)*

"Now you are in direct contact with your subconscious. Your subconscious mind is now ready to accept important ideas. You are very relaxed; your subconscious is open for suggestions now."

(This completes phase two, readying your subconscious to receive the suggestions that you have prepared in advance for it.)

Phase III: Autosuggestion Script for Direct Communication with Your Subconscious and Returning to Normal

When you have arrived at this phase, you will state clearly the suggestions that you have prepared in advance in order to reprogram your subconscious. Statements should be primarily positive, such as, "I will stop preoccupying myself with what might have been and will concentrate on what is," or "Tomorrow's interview will not unnerve me; I am going to perform beautifully." In any case, it is important to prepare your suggestions in advance of beginning any part of this procedure.

After you have entered the suggestion(s) into your subconscious and repeated them several times, tell yourself that you are ready to wake up. Then proceed as follows:

"In a moment, you will be fully awake with your subconscious reprogrammed. I will count from one to five, and with each number you will become more and more aware, you will feel better and better, until I reach five, when you will open your eyes and be fully awake, feeling very refreshed and wonderful. All right. One. Waking up. *(Pause)* Two. More and more refreshed. *(Pause)* Three. Better and better, almost fully awake now. *(Pause)* Four. Feeling very, very good. *(Pause)* And Five. Wide awake."

INDEX